NEW PERSPECTIVES ON NINETEENTH-CENTURY RUSSIAN PROSE

Edited by

George J. Gutsche

and

Lauren G. Leighton

Slavica Publishers, Inc.

Slavica publishes a wide variety of books on the literature, linguistics, languages, folklore, history, and music of Eastern Europe and the USSR. For a complete catalog with prices and ordering information, write to:

Slavica Publishers, Inc.
PO Box 14388
Columbus, Ohio 43214

ISBN: 0-89357-094-X.

This book was published in July, 1982.

Printed in the United States of America.

Dedicated to

J. Thomas Shaw

CONTENTS

PREFACE

The authors of the articles collected here take it for granted that the study of Russian literature is a part of the study of world literature and inseparable from the latter. In this and in other respects they show their indebtedness to and kinship with J. Thomas Shaw who at one time was their teacher at the University of Wisconsin. Any scholarly task undertaken by Shaw or a student of his will find them alert to the literary, esthetic, psychological, and philosophical theories of the West as well as of Eastern Europe, excluding any of the national or ideological provincialism which regrettably vitiates not a few works on both sides of what was once called the iron curtain.

The scholarship practiced and taught by J. Thomas Shaw is firmly rooted in the traditions of philological positivism. The literary text, its genesis, and its interpretation is what this kind of scholarship is concerned with. A sober Kantian dualism is present in it, insisting on a clear separation of what pertains to the subject and his mind, say, Aleksandr Sergeevič Puškin, and what belongs to the object, viz., the text produced by him. The articles in this collection, for the most part, observe this distinction. Wherever they do not, they will meet with the master's censure. Attempts at a monistic esthetic and the maximalism which is its inevitable corollary, whether they may appear in the form of Teutonic mystic idealism, Marxist-Lukacsian dialectics, or even early Šklovskian formalism, do not appeal either to Shaw or to his students.

Shaw, a very fine editor and a scholar thoroughly familiar with the technical aspects of research, writing, and publishing, whose excellent methods course introduced scores of students to the tools and tricks of their trade, could not fail to have had a beneficial influence on the scholarly habits of his disciples. If their publication record is a remarkable one, this may well have something to do with the preparation they received at the Slavic Department of the University of Wisconsin. Each of the articles found in this collection would be a credit to any scholar.

The articles in this volume deal with a variety of subjects, to which they use different approaches. None of them is, strictly speaking, an effort that might be linked directly to the scholarship or influence of J. Thomas Shaw. This is really a credit to him as a teacher, and in happy contrast with the sterile discipleship nurtured by some otherwise excellent scholars and teachers. The articles also show that their authors have freed themselves from the gravitational pull of their dissertations and move about freely in the whole wide space of their field. A look at the subject matter and method of the articles in this collection leaves one impressed with the independence of these young scholars, each of whom has chosen a problem and a method of investigation all his or her own. Nevertheless, one also has the feeling that all of them do speak a common language and will respect each other's work. Such healthy pluralism, yet without even the slightest suspicion of epistemological nihilism or unchecked subjectivity, is very much to the credit of the school from which these young scholars have come.

Shaw's basic conception of scholarship is simple enough. He sees it as analyşis of a literary text, or texts, in the light of a set of facts or of a methodology not previously, or insufficiently, applied to it by other scholars. While simple enough, this conception raises very specific demands: the scholar is asked not only to produce and to assemble facts, but also to organize them into a reasoned whole; and, conversely, he is expected to base his structural observations on secure and complete factual material. I believe that all of the articles here meet these demands. I believe that J. Thomas Shaw will derive considerable satisfaction from this collection.

Victor Terras

INTRODUCTION

Collected here are studies of a variety of writings of best known nineteenth-century Russian authors. Similarities in approach and methodology of the scholars who wrote these studies are to be expected, in view of the background and critical-scholarly training they have shared. Their common concerns include analysis, elucidation, and interpretation of texts which represent generically heterogeneous literary prose: in addition to novels and tales, there are journalistic, historical, and philosophical texts.

No attempt was made to achieve a comprehensive, "representative" view of nineteenth-century prose in Russia. Rather, the goal of the editors was to put together a collection of solid scholarly articles which present original perspectives on specific literary problems which have concerned scholars in the past. That most of the articles deal with Puškin and Dostoevskij is a reflection of the interests and expertise of the contributors.

Contributions are broadly classified, according to emphasis, into those which deal with writers and the ideas of their age, and those which examine comparatively, thematically, or structurally particular literary works.

The authors of these studies take it for granted that the material they are working with and analyzing is worth investigating, and that study of an important writers's work, when based on close readings of that work, can lead to insights that can be tested by reference to the texts themselves. Although the formalist concern for close textual readings and scientific rigor may be discerned in these studies, other concerns should also be apparent: the studies reflect a healthy respect for extrinsic materials (used with appropriate restraints) which contribute to our understanding and appreciation of literature.

Once insights are tested and generalizations demonstrated, our knowledge and understanding of a particular text, the artist's creative techniques, and even the nature of art should be enhanced. Although it is probably true that too great a concern for demonstration, precision, and use of evidence for generalizations can prove tedious and may even stifle the development of provocative new hypotheses, such excessive concern is not evident to us in these studies. They rest on the methodological assumption that true and demonstrable conclusions couched in relatively conventional critical-philological terminology can be interesting and can have value. Of course, questions of methodology usually revolve around questions of value, and what is interesting is often a reflection of values. Given our assumptions and critical frameworks, we believe these studies are interesting and of value. A good part of their appeal is that although they do not display radically new critical techniques, they nonetheless represent solid demonstrations and arguments for looking at Russian texts and authors in new and more rewarding ways. For this reason, we believe they represent valid contributions to our knowledge of Russian literature.

The contributors to this collection have made every effort to relate their work to a wider and now substantial body of writing that constitutes the scholarly tradition for studies of Puškin, Belinskij, Gogol', Turgenev, Dostoevskij, and Tolstoj. As far as possible the studies here have been written so as to contribute something truly new, and at the same time to pay tribute (and show indebtedness where appropriate) to the work of scholars of past and present generations. To ensure the highest level of scholarly thoroughness, the editors have solicited the aid of outside readers — specialists in no other way involved with the collection. Each study has been read and evaluated in draft form for its cogency and its potential as a contribution to world scholarship. Readers were chosen for their established expertise, and were asked to be rigorous in their judgments. We believe the contributions have benefitted from this process.

Four of the studies in this collection are on Puškin; two of these deal with Puškin and other writers (Belinskij and E. T. A. Hoffmann). Gerald Mikkelson examines Puškin's *History of Pugačev* not only for its aesthetic qualities, which have been convincingly demonstrated by Soviet scholars, but also for its distinctiveness as a historical treatise. His principal task is one of interpretation: the polemical qualities of the work are found to be somewhat different from those established by previous scholars. Puškin's central thesis, according to Mikkelson, is that the policies of Peter I and Catherine II which let such social institutions as the old nobility, the *bojarstvo*, decline, were indirectly responsible for, or served as the underlying causes of, the civil disorders of 1773-75 known as the Pugačev rebellion. Furthermore, Puškin did not offer a blanket condemnation (as has been maintained) but rather a selective condemnation of the nobility and military of Catherine's time. Mikkelson's study continues his work on Puškin's historical prose.

The aim of Lauren Leighton's study is to summarize existing scholarship (including his own previous work) and provide a comprehensive judgment of the role of Freemasonry in Puškin's tale "The Queen of Spades." By bringing to the discussion newly found materials on the Masonic rituals and mystical practices used in Russia in Puškin's time, the study puts into perspective various interpretations of the fantastic and realistic aspects of the tale, and also sheds light on its deeper implications, the intertwining of questions of Freemasonry and Puškin's relationship to the Decembrist revolutionary conspiracy. Not only does the study summarize previous investigation of the Masonic connection, it also illuminates the meaning of hidden codes and numerological formulae in the text, using already established evidence and new materials found in Soviet archives.

Puškin's polemical interests are in focus in George Gutsche's study of the poet's journalistic activity in 1836. For a number of reasons, which are explored in the study, Puškin wrote a "letter to the publisher" above the name of a persona — the provincial landowner "A. B." — and had it printed in his own journal *The Contemporary*. Using the device of a letter to himself, he could easily and indirectly deal with a number of issues vital to the survival and success of his journal; these issues related to the journal's editorial direction, its polemical stand in regard to other periodicals of the day, the views of its contributors as distinct from the view of the editor, its opinion of the reading public, and the consistency of its goals. Moreover, with the help of his persona Puškin furthered his negotiations with the young critic Belinskij, whom he planned to recruit. The persona's letter offers an example of Puškin's ingenuity and artistry, for a persona is much like a literary personage, and this study of its contents and functions takes us deep into the world of Russian journalism of the time.

In his study of Tolstoj and Kant, the last contribution in the section devoted to Russian writers in a wider context, Gary Jahn offers a coherent approach and a whole perception of a major nineteenth-century author. In this study he makes particular use of Tolstoj's miscellanies to explore the writer's attitude toward the great German philosopher and illustrate Tolstoj's "applied philosophy." Jahn traces Tolstoj's developing interest in philosophy in general and Kant in particular, documenting the Russian author's sudden change of heart toward Kant after reading *Critique of Practical Reason.* Eventually Tolstoj listed Kant among the great thinkers and teachers of the world, alongside such figures as Buddha, Christ, Spinoza, and Emerson. Jahn's comprehensive study not only contributes to our knowledge of Kant in Russia, but also to our understanding of Tolstoj's philosophical views. Moreover, as Jahn suggests, an understanding of Tolstoj's affinities with Kant can enhance our appreciation of Tolstoj's fiction, since several Kantian notions were used by Tolstoj in his writing, including works written before he recognized how many important ideas he shared with the German thinker.

Roberta Reeder's study of "The Queen of Spades" is the only distinctly structural analysis in the collection. By using a model of analysis indebted to V. A. Propp, the pioneer classifier of Russian folklore, she breaks Puškin's tale into elements which can be compared and contrasted with elements previously derived from similar analyses of E. T. A. Hoffmann's stories. Comparisons and contrasts of elements and configurations of elements from stories by the two authors are shown to yield insights into, and give evidence for, parodistic aspects of "The Queen of Spades." These aspects may have been noted by previous scholars, but they have never been demonstrated so conclusively.

Another basically comparative study is Pierre Hart's examination of Turgenev's tale "First Love" and Dostoevskij's work in the same genre "The Little Hero." Building on his earlier study of Dostoevskij's tale, Hart compares the authors' treatment of a common theme: the awakening of sexual love in troubled male adolescents. The two tales beg for comparisons and contrasts both in character types (boys, fathers, and the women with whom they are involved) and in themes, particularly with respect to the scope and limitations of romantic ideals. The stories are seen as illustrations of the peculiarities and the distinctive features of Turgenev's and Dostoevskij's approach, at a transitional point in their literary development, to rendering significant aspects of emotional experience in art.

Gary Rosenshield also uses a comparative analysis to provide insight into Dostoevskij's fiction. In this case it is Dostoevskij's short novel *Poor Folk* that is analyzed. Again the focus is on characterization, in particular the ways in which Dostoevskij draws the characters of Devuškin and old Pokrovskij. Rosenshield provides specific and very illuminating observations about these characters and their roles in the work, and finds relationships with Gogol' 's Akakij Akakievič of "The Overcoat," who though customarily viewed in relation to Devuškin, turns out in Rosenshield's analysis to share more with Pokrovskij. The analysis of the characters of *Poor Folk* brings us to a deeper understanding of the work, its hero, and its subtextual links to "The Overcoat."

Another Dostoevskij character, the narrator of *The Devils*, is the center of Gene Fitzgerald's study. Analyzing the narrator in his various functions as chronicler, re-creative author, observer, and participant in the novel's action, Fitzgerald discovers new things about Dostoevskij's artistic methods. Each of the novel's narrative perspectives is described and each is associated with or assigned to a particular function. Fitzgerald's aim is to support the view that there is a coherent narrative structure in Dostoevskij's seemingly most biased novel. Fitzgerald suggests that there is no need to hypothesize the existence of two narrative components (for example, a narrative author as opposed to Dostoevskij himself) to make sense of the narrative structure. Fitzgerald's observations go a long way toward clarifying what for scholars has been one of the novel's most perplexing aspects.

Another topic that has intrigued Dostoevskij readers for generations is the nature and function of folklore in his works. Linda Ivanits directs attention to the specific problem of folk beliefs, both Christian and pre-Christian, in *The Brothers Karamazov*. After summarizing existing scholarship on folkloristic and religious allusions in the novel, Ivanits advances a number of interesting hypotheses relating to Father Zosima, the little boy Iljuša, and Smerdjakov. She discusses the meaning of various folk motifs, such as the "unclean force," and demonstrates how important folklore is to the thematic structure of the novel. Like Rosenshield and Fitzgerald, Ivanits here advances an approach to Dostoevskij she has already established in previously published studies, and gives evidence of a wholly thought out perception of Dostoevskij's art.

The editors would like to thank the many scholars who have freely given of their time and expertise to read and offer critical advice concerning the articles in this collection. Their aid was invaluable to us in our efforts to insure that the collection meet the highest possible scholarly standards.

George Gutsche   Lauren Leighton
  Northern Illinois University   University of Illinois at Chicago Circle

PART I

RUSSIAN WRITERS AND THE CULTURAL CONTEXT

PUŠKIN AND FREEMASONRY: "THE QUEEN OF SPADES"

Lauren G. Leighton, University of Illinois at Chicago Circle

> Kak *Pikovaja dama* složna! Sloj
> na sloe.   — Anna Axmatova

Puškin's prose tale "The Queen of Spades" ("Pikovaja dama," 1834) has received as much attention as almost any of his works. Not the least reason for this is the tale's sophistication and complexity. Axmatova was right: each new reading of the work reveals new implications — in themes and motifs, in style, in the complex system of apparent and hidden semantic links among the various parts, in the author's skillful distancing of himself through irony and urbanity, in the conscious literariness and wide-ranging allusions.[1] Not unexpectedly, it is the tale's fantastic side which has attracted the most attention: in the first place, the still debated question as to whether the "secret of the three cards" should be explained rationally or by supernatural means, and then the eccentric accoutrement of setting, the allusions to eighteenth-century mysticism, the Faustian and Napoleonic hero Germann's obsession with the card game, and of course, the ubiquitous numbers associated with every aspect of the tale.[2]

One of the most fruitful studies of the tale deals with it as a parody of the Masonic rite of initiation and the ancient Masonic legend of Hyram-Abif, the purported hero-martyr and builder of King Solomon's temples who died rather than reveal the secrets of the craft. According to this interpretation, by Harry Weber, and to my own additional observations, Germann's stealthy entrance in chapter III into the old countess's mansion, his suspenseful wait for her return from the ball among the eighteenth-century furnishings of her fashionable life sixty years before, and his urgent pleas, three times and again, for the secret that can make his fortune — this carefully arranged ritualistic scene is a reenactment of the Masonic initiate's entrance into the temple and his supplications for the secrets of the craft. The tale is seen as replete with such Masonic symbolism as Germann's third plea on his knees, his plea in the name of himself and three successive generations, the mention of the "appointed hour" and the patterned striking of the clocks, the winding staircase, and the left-right sequences of motion and direction. The Masonic (and Rosicrucian) symbols of rose, Venus, and virgin appear in the tale in the portrait of the young beauty with a rose in her hair and the old countess's cap adorned with roses, in the old woman's reputation in Paris sixty years before as "la Vénus moscovite," and in the jeopardy to the virginity of the heroine Lizaveta Ivanovna by Germann's clandestine courtship. The mystery of the Masonic temple is evoked by the dim green lights, ancient smoothworn chairs along the walls, Chinese wallpaper, portraits painted in Paris by Madame Lebrun, a star, table clocks by Leroy. The mystique of Freemasonry is invoked by allusions to the Masonic mystics and charlatans Count Saint-Germain, Swedenborg, and Casanova.[3]

In a recent article I attempted to demonstrate that this part of the tale contains a series of hidden anagrams, some based on card terminology, some on Masonic, political, and other allusions, and others yielding the name of Puškin's contemporary, the poet Kondratij Ryleev who was hanged in 1826 for his leading role in the political conspiracy which culminated in the revolt of 14 December 1825. This unusual stylistic phenomenon is based on two methods, the first numerical, the second utilizing purely morphological devices such as metathesis and transposition. The general terms for these methods are logomachy and cryptography. The particular method used by Puškin seems to be gematria, the basic system of the Jewish and Christian Cabala according to which cryptograms and cryptonyms are lodged in texts for thaumaturgic or religious purposes. There is no direct evidence that Puškin was versed in gematria, but he is known to have used codes of various sorts, and when he was initiated as a Freemason in 1821 he would have been required to begin learning such thaumaturgic skills as alchemy, cartomancy, numerology, and the Cabala. He would certainly have known that the three key numbers of his tale — three, seven, and one derived from the three magic cards trey, seven, and ace — were developed in the Christian Cabala (the Jewish numbers are three, seven, and twelve), whence they were incorporated into other numerological systems, including the card game Faro, the divination system known as the Tarot, and the symbolism of Masonic rituals. In using this practice to hide the name of Ryleev in the text of his tale, Puškin associated Freemasonry intimately with the Decembrist conspiracy. So far as the question of Decembrism is concerned, it has long been known that the "Gambler's Song" which serves as the tale's epigraph is a parody on the "Agitational Songs" of Ryleev and his fellow Decembrist Aleksandr Bestužev-Marlinskij. Puškin was obsessed with the fate of his Decembrist friends, especially with the execution of the five principal leaders. Ryleev and Puškin were Masonic brothers, and by lodging the Decembrist's name secretly in the text of his tale, Puškin could honor his brother in a unique and intimate way. Gematria perhaps enabled him to exorcise his mind of memories too painful to be expressed overtly and too controversial to pass the censor.[4]

We know very little about Puškin as a Freemason, and although we know a great deal more about his relationships with the Decembrists, the conspiratorial nature of the affair left us with almost as many questions as answers about his role.[5] Nevertheless, the Masonic orientation of "The Queen of Spades," especially the evidence of such a sophisticated practice as gematria, suggests that Puškin was more carefully learned in Freemasonry than has been appreciated, and the question becomes all the more interesting because of the many implications and allusions present in the text of the tale. There is no need to suggest that Puškin was inordinately adept in the secrets of the Masonic craft or that the Freemasons of his time were generally erudite as regards thaumaturgic practices, but the few known facts of his Masonic activities are consistently associated with political, Decembrist matters, and there is additional evidence, some of it available in published sources, some in unpublished archival materials, which shows that he was more closely versed in such practices as gematria than has been appreciated.

According to one of his diaries, Puškin was initiated into the Kišinev lodge of Ovid on 4 May 1821.[6] The lodge, which was obedient to the Grand Lodge of Astraea, was closed with all other lodges in Russia by order of Alexander I on 12 August 1822. The reasons for the ban on Freemasonry are still not fully understood, but Puškin once claimed that the chief reason was the political activity of his own lodge. In a letter of 1826 to the older poet V. A. Žukovskij, who was working to clear Puškin of complicity in the Decembrist conspiracy, Puškin asserted: "I was a Mason of the Kišinev Lodge, that is, the one because of which all lodges in Russia were ruined. I, finally, was in contact with the majority of the present conspirators [the Decembrists]." Although Puškin is generally believed to have exaggerated here, the lodge of Ovid was intensely political. Its Master, P. S. Puščin, was a political activist, as was another leading member, Puščin's mentor and commander, M. F. Orlov. Puškin and Puščin exchanged poems based on Masonic symbolism at this time.[7]

Puškin would not have ceased to be a Freemason simply because the lodges were closed in 1822: the disclosure of the secrets of the craft during the rite of initiation is a lifetime, symbolically irrevocable commitment. It is not likely that Puškin was active as a Freemason for any extended period of time, but he would have been free to participate in Masonic work in any of the foreign embassies and consulates he frequented in the later 1820s and 1830s. And when he turned to the writing of "The Queen of Spades" in 1833, his initiation of 1821 had given him the right and the duty to seek out Masonic knowledge of the sort that is evident in the text of his tale. That Puškin was still interested in Freemasonry and able to express himself in Masonic symbols is indicated by a letter of 1833. In a letter of 5 March to M. P. Pogodin, attempting to persuade the historian to join him in his own historical research in state archives, Puškin promised: "You will perform such marvels that we and our posterity will pray for you as we pray for Schloetzer and Lomonosov." Pogodin immediately recognized this as an allusion to the legend of Hyram-Abif, for he replied: "But let them sing my memory, but let them cut out my tongue in as many strips as they wish!" (PSS, XV, 53, 57; see also Weber, 446-47.) Puškin's reference to the prayers of posterity has to do with the Masonic initiate's received obligation to revere the great Masonic hero-martyr (and to remember all fallen brothers). It is quite similar to Germann's oath to the countess in chapter III that he and three successive generations of his descendants will revere her memory and pray for her soul. Pogodin's reply continues the ritualistic recitation: he will preserve the secrets of the archives as Hyram-Abif preserved the secrets of the Masonic craft.

As Weber has shown, the most distinct parallels between Freemasonry and "The Queen of Spades" are to be found in the symbolism of the initiation ritual. Citing descriptions of the ritual by such scholars of Russian Freemasonry as A. N. Pypin and Tira Sokolovskaja,[8] he notes that asking the time, as someone asks the absent-minded Germann in chapter VI, is essential to the ritual; that the chairs lined in "sorrowful symmetry" along the walls of the old countess's mansion correspond to the symmetrical orientation of the officers of the lodge along the walls of the temple; that the receipt of a key, as when Lizaveta Ivanovna gives Germann the key so that he can leave by the hidden staircase, is a symbol of the receipt of the secrets of the craft; that the sequence of the hero's pleas during his confrontation with the countess in chapter III is identical to the Masonic initiate's supplications; and that the guests at the ball in chapter IV even pay their respects to the old woman as if "in accordance with an established ritual." Other correspondences are the countess's "galvanic" motions of the head swaying to the left and right as compared to the use of galvanic devices to govern the movements of a skeleton in the decor of at least one Russian lodge; the similarities between the names of the characters Čaplickij and Čekalinskij in the tale and those of the prominent Freemasons Čaplic and Čekalevskij; and the fact that the director of the Obuxovskij Hospital, where Germann ends his days, was the controversial Masonic leader Dr. Georg Heinrich Ellisen. There is even a parallel between the ritual phrase, "that which my soul yearns for, but does not attain" ("čego žaždet, no ne postigaet, duša moja"), and Lizaveta Ivanovna's realization about Germann, "Money, that is what his soul yearns for!" ("Den'gi, vot čego alkala ego duša!"). (Weber, 436-42.)

Weber's research is further substantiated by Sokolovskaja's other studies of Masonic rituals and symbolism. In a description of the St. John's Rituals, which would include the initiation ritual,[9] she mentions a number of features which are also present in the tale or correspond in symbolism to features in the tale. These include a three-cornered lampholder, the placement of three symbolic lamps, sometimes in groups of three,[10] dim lights and shadow, striking clocks, three knocks on the door of the temple by which the doorkeeper asks permission to enter with the initiate, and "a staircase which leads to heaven." Relevant here to Weber's suggestion that Puškin's references to staircases imply the symbolic staircases of Freemasonry is Sokolovskaja's observation that the initiation ritual is called "the first step of the Masonic staircase" to perfection. The staircase has seven steps, each symbolizing a Masonic virtue. She notes also that when the initiate has made the important decision to become a Freemason, after being given three chances to turn back, the Master of the lodge declares: "Your fate has been decided!" ("Žrebij vaš rešilsja!"). ("Obrjadnost' vol'nyx kamenščikov," 80-98.) This, too has its parallel in Puškin's tale, in the narrator's statement at the end of chapter II: "That minute decided his fate!" ("Eta minuta rešila ego učast'!").[11]

In a study of the ideology and symbolism of Freemasonry, Sokolovskaja devotes attention to a special Masonic sign which has a place in "The Queen of Spades" - the crossing of arms over the breast. All three main characters of the tale are depicted with their arms crossed this way at important moments: Lizaveta Ivanovna, when Germann enters her bedroom in chapter IV; Germann, as he sits in the window in the same scene; and the old countess, in her coffin in chapter V. According to Sokolovskaja, the crossing of arms was a secret sign of Masonic identification and a plea for help. She relates the story of the Decembrist Baten'kov who was saved from death when French officers, who turned out to be Masonic brothers, found him unconscious on the battlefield with his arms crossed over his breast, inadvertently in the Masonic form (*Russkoe masonstvo,* 82). In a study of Russian Rosicrucianism Sokolovskaja describes a ceremony in which such gestures are performed as the crossing of arms and kneeling in supplication. Two brothers also place their hands on each other's shoulders, their arms crossed. In these ceremonies the symbolism has to do with both the cross as a form and the Crucifixion from which the form was derived. It would also have to do with the rose and cross of Rosicrucianism.[12]

Russian scholars of Freemasonry, as scholars of the craft elsewhere, had considerable difficulty sorting out the rituals of the various Masonic systems, and they failed to identify the precise texts of the rituals employed in Russia. The observation of each step of a ritual is of great importance in guaranteeing adeptness in the craft, and the matter of the integrity of the texts has always been a source of controversy in the history of Freemasonry. As Weber notes, this makes it difficult to identify which ritual Puškin might have adhered to in the writing of "The Queen of Spades" (436-37). The text Puškin would have known, and been required to memorize, would most likely have been the one authorized by the Grand Lodge of Astraea, to which his own Kišinev lodge of Ovid was obedient during its brief existence.[13] Complete reliable texts were apparently not available to the leading scholars of Russian Freemasonry, but fortunately, several texts have survived in the archives of the Institute of Russian Literature (Puškin House) of the Academy of Sciences in Leningrad. Puškin's lodge was the only lodge subordinate to the Grand Lodge of Astraea which was authorized to use the Scottish Rite, and texts and other documents of this rite are also preserved in the archives of Puškin House. A comparison of these materials with those of the other lodges, which adhered to the Swedish or to the Ancient English systems, shows that while there are important textual differences, the basic symbolic elements of Freemasonry are common to all the texts. Taken together, the various documents provide still further evidence of Puškin's use of Masonic elements in his tale.[14]

Among the allegorical images illustrated in one document, for example, are seven candles in three holders, crossed ladders with seven rungs each, and the signs for the seven positive qualities of Freemasonry. A plan for the arrangement of a "third chamber" in the same document shows a coffin, a triangular table surrounded by seven flames, and a candelabra with seven candles.[15] A text of the rituals for opening and closing the lodge, and for the initiation of new members, shows many of the features mentioned by Pypin, Sokolovskaja, and Weber: three knocks on a door or, at prescribed moments, on a table; questions and answers in sequences of three; a request for the time; three symbolic journeys around the temple in order to, among other purposes, assure the sanctity of the temple has not been violated; the arrangement of the officers of the lodge in four directions along the walls; the presentation by the Master of the lodge or one of the two Wardens of the three signs and the seven Masonic virtues, repeated in the Master's injunctions to the initiate.[16]

One aspect of the initiation ritual which appears throughout the archival documents and is particularly relevant to "The Queen of Spades" is the seven injunctions regarding the virtues by which every Freemason must guide himself and be guided by his brothers to perfection. The documents show that the initiate visits the temple three times in supplication and is three times on each visit offered opportunity to turn back. When he asserts his resolve the third time on the third visit, once on his knees, he is accepted into the brotherhood by the symbolic act of accepting the secrets of the craft as they are revealed to him by the Master. Among the most important of these are the seven virtues, which according to one document are discrétion, obéisance, les bonnes moeurs, l'amour de l'humanité, principalement des frères, persévérance ou courage, générosité ou désintérestement, and l'amour de la mort. Other texts substitute or add modération and tempérance to discrétion, add patience to obéisance and religion to les bonnes moeurs, and substitute espérance for persévérance.[17] The document listing the seven virtues with their signs gives them as tempérance, fortitude, foy, espérance, prudence, justice, charité (No. 51). In one variant or the other these virtues are important to "The Queen of Spades." Three of them are professed by Germann in his favorite saying: "No! Calculation, moderation, and industrious-ness: these are my three trusty cards: this is what will triple, multiply seven-fold my capital and bring me peace and independence" ("Net! rasčet, umerennost' i trudoljubie: vot moi tri vernye karty, vot čto utroit, usemerit moj kapital i dostavit mne pokoj i nezavisimost'!"). Certainly there is great irony in Puškin's substitution of calculation (rasčet) for discrétion and independence (neza-visimost') for obéisance, and joining them with moderation and industriousness (trudoljubie; espérance, persévérance). Ironic also is the fact that the Masonic virtues les bonnes moeurs and religion are present in the still unidentified epigraph to chapter IV: "Homme sans moeurs et sans religion!" And Germann's prudence, his desire for peace, and all the irony of his stealthy invasion of the old countess's home are paralleled in a warning issued by the Second (Junior) Warden during the revelation of the seven virtues: "Nous avons été calme, car nous avons travaillé, nous avons été secret car aucun profane n'a pu s'approcher des nous, nous avons été prudens, car nous avons gardé l'entrée de notre temple" (No. 105).

A particularly interesting aspect of "The Queen of Spades" has to do with the tale's hidden anagrams, the use of the cabalistic practice of gematria. Such thaumaturgic practices were common among Freemasons in all countries (Mackey, I, 54-55), and literary Freemasons — Goethe, for example — carried Masonic practices over quite easily into their writings ("Gematria in 'The Queen of Spades,'" 457). Puškin frequently used codes and similar practices in his literary works, particularly as a means of expressing his thoughts about the Decembrist conspiracy, and the encoding of Ryleev's name in the text of his tale was for him a serious matter both literarily and personally. There is no evidence that he knew the practice, but as has been shown, he would have been required to learn the Cabala, numerology, and magic when he became an Apprentice Mason. The anagrams are contained in chapter III of the tale, in the passage where Germann waits outside the old countess's home. The strand of seven words beginning with the first twenty-one words (3 X 7) of the paragraph are:

veter vyl, mokryj sneg padal xlop'jami; fonari

The first three and the seventh words of this strand produce the syllables:

ve ter vyl mo kryj fo na ri

Through transposition and metathesis of these syllables they work out to the name Kondratij F. Ryleev (*ko nra ti f ry le ev*). Among the other anagrams which break out to the name of Ryleev are:

fonari svetilis' tusklo ulicy byli pusty izredka
van'ka na toščej kljače svoej vysmatrivaja zapozdalogo sedoka
nakonec grafininu karetu podali germann videl kak lakei vynesli pod ruki
raboty slavnogo *leroy* korobočki ruletki veera i raznye damskie
    igruški izobretennye v konce
ryxlomu snegu švejcar zaper dveri okna pomerkli

The practice of gematria was introduced into Russia in the eighteenth century by the Russian Freemasons most greatly influenced by Rosicrucianism. The man who brought the practice to the Russian brethren and prescribed it to them in a curious instruction was Baron G. Ja. Schroeder, a controversial figure in the circle of Rosicrusians centered around V. I. Novikov. His instruction reads as follows:

Wenn ein RK [Rosen Kreuzer] stirbt, muss sein Wappen eingesandt werden, und jeder RK muss während jeder Minute seines Lebens solche Anstallten, mit den geheimen Schriften treffen, dass nicht ein Blätchen davon bey dem aller schleunigsten Todesfall in fremde Hände kömmt, welches noch der Ruhe seiner Seelen (sic), wenn sie

nicht schon ganz rein abgeschieden, Schaden bringen kann. Diess
muss jedem Junior schon eingeprägt werden. . .[18]

That is, it is the duty of every brother to ensure that the "secret writings" do
not fall into the wrong hands. As Mackey indicates, cryptography is no longer
used by Freemasons to protect the secrets of the craft — no cryptographic
system can withstand modern methods of breaking codes. But in Puškin's day
codes were a standard practice of Freemasonry, and they provided all kinds of
unusual devices for literary works.[19] For Puškin, gematria was one more practice
— together with numerology, cartomancy, covert allusions, ironic twists of
meaning, and cruel tricks of fate — by which to make "The Queen of Spades"
one of the most intriguing works in all world literature.

"The Queen of Spades" is, in fact, a highly complex and intriguing literary
work which had provoked more speculation than any other of his works. It lends
itself to interpretation, and it is so intricately, so deliberately ambiguous that the
scholarship devoted to it is markedly ingenious. In a recent attempt to interpret
again the supernatural aspects of "The Queen of Spades" Diana Lewis Burgin
neatly articulates how Puškin was able to invite so much speculation about the
tale:

> In order to make the supernatural credible, to suspend momentarily
> the reader's disbelief and draw him into the mystery of his tale,
> Puškin employs the narrative device of mystification. He plays upon
> certain events and characters in such a way as to make them seem
> strange and mysterious when they are not, and, conversely, he
> de-emphasizes or mocks those mystifying and supernatural events. . .
> which are clues to the real mystery. Using the device of mystifica-
> tion as a veil for his supernatural mystery, Puškin creates in the
> reader ambivalence about the reality of irrational occurrences, so
> that he can, with ample justification in the text, interpret the story
> in several ways. . .[20]

This device of mystification — the deliberate ambiguity which entices the reader
to speculation — can even be taken one step further. For no sooner does what
seems important in the tale turn out to be insignificant, and the de-emphasized
or mocked become central and serious, than the process is again reversed — the
important that turns out to be unimportant is again given import, and what has
been de-emphasized or ridiculed, only to be suddenly revealed as significant, is
again shunted aside by irony.

This constantly shifting complexity — in which Puškin takes obvious delight
— is nowhere more evident than in regard to the Masonic aspects of "The Queen
of Spades." Freemasonry is so carefully de-emphasized in the tale as to be
detected only by a practiced Freemason; yet once the Masonic aspects are

revealed, they turn up in clue after clue, in words and phrases, and in the decoding of the hidden text, until Freemasonry is revealed to be a main theme. Yet, even when Freemasonry is fully revealed, it is by no means clear how seriously it is to be taken. As Weber has shown, the tale is in many ways a parody of Freemasonry — what would seem to be serious matters are mocked. And when Freemasonry is shown to be associated in the tale with a wide range of cabalistic, thaumaturgic practices — the whole question of number and numerology — Puškin's delight in word and number games, in astounding coincidences, and in just plain spoofing subjects Freemasonry to outright ridicule. No sooner does this become apparent, however, that Puškin creates still another ambivalence by introducing the question of the Decembrist conspiracy and the fate of Kondratij Ryleev — a question which he would never consider to be a matter of humorous consideration. Truly, as Axmatova has stated, "The Queen of Spades" is a sophisticated, multi-meaninged, multi-leveled work of art whose full implications we have not yet begun to appreciate. Layer by layer, it yields more questions, impressing on us once again just how complex is the art of Puškin.

NOTES

1. For Axmatova's statement see Lidija Čukovskaja, *Zapiski ob Anne Axmatovoj*, vol. I (Paris: YMCA Press, 1976), 21.

2. For an attempt to provide an exhaustive survey of the fantastic elements of the tale see my "Numbers and Numerology in 'The Queen of Spades,'" *Canadian Slavonic Papers*, 19 (1977), 417-43, and extensive citations there.

3. Harry B. Weber, *"Pikovaja dama:* A Case for Freemasonry in Russian Literature," *Slavic and East European Journal*, 12 (1968), 435-47.

4. Lauren G. Leighton, "Gematria in 'The Queen of Spades': A Decembrist Puzzle," *Slavic and East European Journal*, 21 (1977), 455-69. Stephen L. Baehr, "The Masonic Component in Eighteenth-Century Russian Literature," in *Russian Literature in the Age of Catherine the Great*, ed. Anthony Cross (Oxford: Willem A. Meeuws, 1976), 121-39, demonstrates that Masonic codes were used often in eighteenth-century Russian literature and that "these codes supposedly communicate ineffable knowledge that cannot be translated into normal human words. . ." For an account of Puškin's obsession with finding the graves of the martyred Decembrists see Anna Axmatova, "Puškin i nevskoe vzmor'e," *O Puškine: Stat'i i zametki* (Moscow: Sov. pisatel', 1977).

5. For a thorough review of the evidence of Puškin's relationship to the Decembrist movement see B. S. Mejlax, "Puškin v xode sledstvija i suda nad dekabristami," *Puškin i ego èpoxa* (Moscow: GIXL, 1958), 345-62.

6. A. S. Puškin, *Polnoe sobranie sočinenij* (17 vols.; M.,L.: AN SSSR, 1937-59), XII, 303.

7. See T. G. Cjavlovskaja, "Otkliki na sud'by dekabristov v tvorčestve Puškina," in *Literaturnoe nasledie dekabristov*, ed. V. G. Bazanov and V. E. Bacuro (Leningrad: Nauka, 1975), 204-05, and V. I. Semevskij, "Dekabristy-Masony," *Minuvšie gody*, March (18), 162-69.

8. Research in Freemasonry was conducted largely in the years between the 1860s and 1917, and the level of scholarship is appreciably high. See A. N. Pypin, *Russkoe masonstvo: XVIII i pervaja četvert' XIX v.* (Petrograd: Ogni, 1916); T. O. Sokolovskaja, "Masonskie sistemy," in *Masonstvo v ego prošlom i nastojaščem*, ed. S. P. Mel'gunov and M. P. Sidorov (2 vols.; Moscow: Zadruga/ K. F. Nekrasov, 1915), II, 52-59; "Obrjadnost' vol'nyx kamenščikov," *Ibid.*, 80-117; and *Russkoe masonstvo i ego značenie v istorii obščestvennogo dviženija* (St. Petersburg: N. Glagolev, 1908).

9. The first three Masonic degrees, common to all Masonic orders, are called Symbolic Degrees and Craft Degrees because they are based on the symbolism of architecture and building. They are also called Primitive, to denote their supposed ancient origin, Scottish (Ecossais) to signify the supposed revival of ancient Freemasonry in Scotland, and St. John Degrees in honor of the patron of Freemasons.

10. According to Albert G. Mackey, *An Encyclopedia of Freemasonry*, new and rev. ed. (2 vols.; Chicago-New York-London: The Masonic History Co., 1924), II, 513, the number nine, known as the triple trinity, is among the most powerful Masonic numbers. No matter what number is multiplied by nine, it can be manipulated back to nine. Thus, $9 \times 9 = 81$ $(8+1 = 9)$; $9 \times 8 = 72$ $(7+2 = 9)$, and so on; $9 \times 371 = 3339$ $(3+3+3+9 = 18; 1+8 = 9)$. The number works out neatly for numerological purposes in a basic schema such as 9 18 27 36 45 54 63 72 81 90. As can be seen, the first numbers reading forward are 9 1 2 3 4 5 6 7 8, while the second numbers reading backwards are 0 1 2 3 4 5 6 7 8 9, and each double number when added yields 9. For Puškin's use of the numerical combination in "The Queen of Spades" see "Numbers and Numerology in 'The Queen of Spades,'" 422, 423.

11. "My fate has been decided!" is a Romantic cliche, and therefore this could be an affinity rather than a particular Masonic parallel. Kondratij Ryleev used essentially the same formula in his last letter to his wife just before his execution: "God and Sovereign have decided my fate" ("Bog i Gosudar' rešili učast' moju").

12. T. O. Sokolovskaja, "Brat'ja zlatorozovogo kresta (K istorii rozenkrejcerstva v Rossii)," *Russkij arxiv,* 1906, No. 9, 89-93.

13. See the chronological directory of the Russian lodges appended to Pypin, *Russkoe masonstvo;* also available in A. N. Pypin, *Xronologičeskij ukazatel' russkix lož ot pervogo vvedenija masonstva do zapreščenija ego. 1731-1822* (St. Petersburg, 1873).

14. The Masonic holdings of Puškin House are preserved in Razdel II, opis' 2, and include ninety manuscripts numbered from 51 to 140. They are about equally divided between texts of rites and documents prescribing such mystical practices as alchemy, divination, and cabalistic interpretations. They are almost all manuscripts of the Grand Lodge of Astraea, Orient of Petersburg, 1815-22. Among the most important documents are detailed membership lists.

15. No. 51, "Allegoričeskie izobraženija v odežde i v obstanovke masonov."

16. No. 105, "Obrjady otkrytija i zakrytija masonskix zasedanij. Obrjady priema novyx členov."

17. No. 105; see also No. 102, "Nastavlenija k želajuščemu vstupit' v obrjad svob. kamenščikov," No. 104, "Ustanovlenija Šotlandskix lož o prinjatii tovarišča i drugie instrukcii, tetradi No. 1-5, 7," and No. 109, "Akty pervyja stepeni svobodnogo kamenščičestva. Masonskie pravila s tolkovanijami. Obrjady prinjatija v raznye stepeni. Ob"jasnenija allegorii. Pesny. Tomy 1-4."

18. Ja. L. Barskov, ed., *Perepiska moskovskix masonov XVIII-go veka (1780-1792 gg.)* (Petrograd: Imp. Ak. Nauk, 1915), 227. Barskov identifies Heinrich Jacob Schroeder (1757-97?) as a Prussian adventurer who attempted to assume the mantle of the recently deceased Masonic leader Schwartz. He exerted an influence on the Moscow Rosicrucians I. V. Lopuxin, I. V. Turgenev, A. M. Kutuzov, and P. A. Ratiščev, and worked closely with N. I. Novikov in his publishing enterprises. Many of the Masonic rites introduced into Russia in the 1780s were brought by Schroeder. The instruction was printed in Russian translation in P. P. Pekarskij, "Dopolnenija k istorii masonstva v Rossii XVIII stoletija," *Sbornik statej, čitannyx v otdelenii russkogo jazyka i slovesnosti Imp. ak. nauk,* VII, No. 4 (1909), 87. Pekarskij did not know that the signature "Sacerdos" was Schroeder's Masonic name, and therefore identified the work as "the diary of an unknown Rosicrucian."

19. For a discussion of this problem and a study of another use of such practices by a Decembrist writer see Lauren G. Leighton, "Bestuzhev-Marlinskii's 'The Frigate Hope': A Decembrist Puzzle," *Canadian Slavonic Papers,* (1980), 171-86.

20. Diana Lewis Burgin, "The Mystery of 'Pikovaja dama': A New Interpretation," in *Mnemozina: Studia litteraria russica in honorem Vsevolod Setchkarev,* ed. Joachim T. Baehr and Norman W. Ingham (Munich: Wilhelm Fink, 197), 56.

PUŠKIN'S *HISTORY OF PUGAČEV:* THE LITTÉRATEUR AS HISTORIAN

Gerald E. Mikkelson, University of Kansas

No picture of Aleksandr Puškin's genius as a man of letters can be complete without considering his many historical research activities and writings. An astonishingly large part of his corpus consists of works in every mode and genre which reflect (or, more exactly, refract) to a greater or lesser degree the author's life-long preoccupation with the stuff of history — especially of his own native Russia. And in the final period of his life — the 1830's — Puškin made a serious attempt to add to the laurels of poet, dramatist, and prose writer, that of the historian. Both the reactions of his contemporaries and the research of 19th- and 20th-century Puškin scholars confirm that Puškin achieved considerable success in this endeavor.[1]

Puškin is now usually assigned a respectable place in the early development of modern Russian historiography.[2] This reputation would undoubtedly be even greater had he lived long enough to complete his work on the reign of Peter the Great.[3] As it is, Puškin's achievement as a historian can best be judged on the basis of his only finished work of historical writing — *A History of Pugačev* (*Istorija Pugačeva;* written 1833, published 1834).[4]

In a work which (in other hands) could have become a dry recapitulation of campaigns and skirmishes, one is struck in reading *Istorija Pugačeva* by the extent to which Puškin remains the consummate literary stylist. "In striving for artistic expressiveness . . . [he] applied methods characteristic of literary creativity." (Ovč., 150.) Vivid and colorful action depicted in concise, tightly constructed sentences which are propelled forward by the frequent use of adverbial participles (for example, *uvidja konnitsu, brosja puški*), lend to Puškin's narrative a pithiness and dynamism matched only by his mature fiction, such as *The Captain's Daughter.*[5] "In this way," writes Ovčinnikov, "Puškin reformed the style of scholarly historical writing — by making it resemble to some degree artistic prose. In Puškin's creative genius the gifts of the great artist and the talented research historian [*istorik-istočnikoved*] were organically merged." (Ovč., 150.)

Not only in the stylistic sense were literary esthetic purposes involved in Puškin's writing of *A History of Pugačev.* His earliest adumbrations of the Pugačev motif are found in the unfinished adventure tale "Dubrovskij," in the unfinished novel in verse "Ezerskij, " and in the first schematic outlines for the historical prose novel *The Captain's Daughter,* all dated 1832, almost one year before he wrote *A History of Pugačev.* These three highly dissimilar literary projects have in common the centrality of the themes of the gentry pariah and his kindred association with the *narod.* Recognizing that an "artistic portrayal of the peasant war required its prior historical study" (Ovč., 14.), Puškin interrupted his work on these three narratives and became engrossed in research on the Pugačev uprising.[6] In *A History of Pugačev,* one finds a detailed and unembellished account of the combined rebellion of Yaik Cossacks and other non-gentry social groupings against socio-political oppression.

Although most Puškin scholars, including the historians, agree that *The Captain's Daughter* is more significant than and "superior" to *A History of Pugačev,*[7] it would be unfair to Puškin the historian to regard his monograph as nothing more than a preliminary sketch for the novel. For *A History of Pugačev* belongs, despite its "literariness," to historical discourse; and it withstands the most intense scrutiny as an independent historiographical treatise. Although *The Captain's Daughter* augments full appreciation of *A History of Pugačev,* Puškin was able in the latter not only to write a straightforward account of "military operations until then virtually unknown,"[8] but also to bring before the eyes of the public a strikingly original and bold interpretation of the revolt. Recent Soviet scholarship has demonstrated that Puškin tried in his first large historiographical undertaking to provide a clear, detailed, and objective account of the military events connected with the war. However, the analysis here suggests that *A History of Pugačev* has also a distinctly polemical basis and that its contents are continually informed and interpreted by Puškin's view of Russian history, especially that of the eighteenth century. The central tenet of this view is the conviction that, however illustrious Peter I and Catherine II may have been as historical figures, their policies and those of the lesser monarchs reigning between them, led to the downfall of two venerable institutions, the Russian *bojarstvo,* and, coincidentally, an autonomous, though loyal, Yaik Cossackdom. Quite daringly, without mincing words, Puškin places principal blame for the civil catastrophe of 1773-75 not upon the insurgents, but upon the government and upon the nobility, which was the mainstay of the government's authority throughout the land.[9] Thus, in its essential respects, *A History of Pugačev* represents a continuation of the main ideas set forth by Puškin in his 1822 essay "On Russian History of the Eighteenth Century." In that essay, while all the Imperial reigns beginning with Peter I are said to have contributed to the decline and fall of the Russian nobility and of Russian national life in general, no single monarch is accused of having made a more destructive impact than Catherine upon the mores and fabric of Russian society. *A History of Pugačev* proves that the author's youthful view of the structure of Catherine's Russia as essentially decadent was never abandoned. Moreover, the treatise serves as an illustration of how very close the Russian Empire came to being toppled in 1773-74 by the so-called "Pugačevščina." All of the foregoing conclusions are summarized by Puškin in the final paragraph of his narrative which begins:

> And so ended the revolt, which was started by a handful of disobedient Cossacks, strengthened through the unpardonable negligence of the authorities and which shook the state from Siberia to

Moscow and from the Kuban' to the forests of Murom. Complete
tranquility was not established for a long time. Panin and Suvorov
remained for a whole year in the subdued provinces, strengthening in
them the debilitated rule, restoring the cities and forts and rooting
out the last sprigs of the suppressed rebellion. (IX, 80-81.)

Especially illuminating in this regard is Chapter I of *A History of Pugačev,*
in which Puškin concisely summarizes the origins and history of the Yaik (Ural)
Cossacks and their changing relationship to the central Russian power, whether
in Moscow or in St. Petersburg. According to this account, the eighteenth-
century Russian governments, especially those of Peter I and Catherine II,
conducted a cruel and relentless campaign to destroy the indigenous military,
political, and economic institutions of the Yaik Cossacks and to subordinate this
proud and independent people to the aims of an autocratic central government.[10]

The point of view expressed in *A History of Pugačev* about the eighteenth-
century emperors and empresses of Russia and about the overall effect of their
reigns upon the condition of the state is essentially the same as that which
Puškin had expressed in his essay "On Russian History of the Eighteenth
Century" of 1822 and his various remarks of 1830 on this subject: that the
policies of Peter I and his successors had tended to undermine the freedom and
power of independent social institutions and groupings; and that such "cruel"
(IX, 9.) measures were, in the main, deleterious in their effects upon the Russian
state.

In most of the relevant writings, such as his "Notes on the Russian
Nobility" of 1830, Puškin had emphasized the declining fortunes of the
dvorjanstvo and, by implication, of the whole Russian people in the eighteenth
century. In *A History of Pugačev,* the focus shifts, at least initially, to another
social grouping, the Yaik Cossacks. But the principle is the same. The autonomy
and distinctive way of life of the Yaik Cossacks had been destroyed by the
Russian government.

A History of Pugačev shows that the Yaik Cossacks were goaded into
rebellion by the Russian government's deliberate and century-long campaign to
absorb the area and its people into the Russian Empire proper. While the work is
devoted mainly to a detailed, chronological account of the principal military
actions of 1773-74, it also documents how poorly prepared the Russian government and army were to meet such an emergency at that time and how vulnerable
the Russian population itself was to the appeals of such an audacious civil
uprising.

Pugačev's forces, within two months after their initial uprising in the village
of Yaitsk, had grown to number around twenty-five thousand. In Puškin's
words:

Their nucleus was comprised of Yaik Cossacks and soldiers taken from various forts. But around them there had accumulated an unbelievable number of Tartars, Bashkirs, Kalmyks, rebellious peasants, runaway convicts, and all manner of tramps. (IX, 26.)

In referring to this human potpourri in aggregate, Puškin often used conventional deprecatory terms such as *svoloč'* and *čern'* (meaning "the rabble"). However, he repeatedly stresses the ease with which these masses were aroused and won over to the side of the rebellion and the contempt in which they held their gentry masters and the ruling government officials in their areas. In this sense, Puškin's *A History of Pugačev* was hardly designed to reassure its Russian gentlemen readers.

Everywhere that Pugačev's army went, it was greeted with bread-and-salt (*xleb-sol'*) not only by the common people, but also by intermediate strata, such as priests and merchants and petty government functionaries, while the noblemen usually fled for their lives. According to Puškin, this pattern especially held true in the summer of 1774, after Pugačev had crossed over to the west side of the Volga into Russia proper and was heading, for a time, in the direction of Moscow. Puškin writes:

> Pugačev's crossing produced general consternation. The whole western side of the Volga rose up and went over to the pretender. Peasant serfs rioted; adherents of other faiths and the newly christened began to kill off the Russian priests. The province chiefs fled from their cities, the noblemen from their estates; both were caught in flight by the rabble and delivered by them from everywhere to Pugačev. Pugačev decreed freedom for the *narod,* the extermination of the gentry, the removal of tax levies, and the free distribution of salt. (IX, 68-69.)

Numerous other passages could be cited from the work, indicating a positive reception for Pugačev at Penza and other towns along the path of his advance. It is no doubt true, as Puškin suggests in one place, that the villagers often capitulated as much from fear as from strong pro-rebel sympathies. They knew that Pugačev was being pursued and that his army would not remain in their region for more than a day or so. This instinctive pragmatism, regardless of true sympathies, is reflected in Puškin's remark that: "the *narod* often did not know to whom they should give their allegiance. To the question: Whom do you recognize as ruler, Petr Fedorovič [Pugačev] or Ekaterina Alekseevna [Catherine]? — peaceful people did not dare to answer without knowing to which side their questioners belonged." (IX, 74.)

However, Puškin makes it very clear that the sympathies of the *narod* and of other social groups as well were overwhelmingly on the side of the insurgents.

The wrath of the civil insurrection was directed specifically against the high-ranking resident agents of the government and against the landed gentry.[11]

General Aleksandr Il'ič Bibikov, who did not even live to see the worst of the rebellion, seems however to have clearly discerned its potential dangers. Puškin quotes a letter to Denis Fonvizin from Kazan' on January 29, 1774, in which Bibikov writes:

> I am hourly concerned and I will employ every means in order to eradicate the spirit of unrest and rebellion which has inundated such an expanse. We have begun everywhere to thrash the villains, but these locusts have multiplied unbelievably. I do not despair of trouncing them, but to quiet the almost universal agitation of the rabble presents great difficulties. It is made most inconvenient of all by the great extent of this evil. But the Lord's will be done! I am doing and will do what I can. Will this accursed mob come to its senses? You know Pugačev is not what is important; what is important is the universal indignation. And Pugačev is but a toy dummy being played with by the thieving Yaik Cossacks. (IX, 201.)[12]

Puškin makes his own most revealing statement on this matter in one of his "General Remarks" transmitted to Nicholas I through Count Benkendorf in January 1835, one month after the initial publication of the *History*.[13] Puškin writes:

> All the common people [*Ves' černyj narod*] were for Pugačev. They were given encouragement by the clergy, not only by the priests and monks, but also by the father superiors and the bishops. Only the nobility was openly on the side of the government. Pugačev and his collaborators at first wanted to win even the nobility over to their side, but their interests were too antithetical. (N.B. The class of scriveners and pettifoggers was still small and belonged decisively to the common people. The same can be said about officers who had risen through the ranks. Many of the latter were in Pugačev's bands, Švanvič alone was from a real gentry background [*iz xorošix dvorjan*].)[14] (IX, 375.)

Vladimir Mavrodin is perfectly correct in saying that "the sympathies of the author of the book [*A History of Pugačev*] were on the side of the *narod*, which had risen up in a struggle for its rights."[15] However, Mavrodin, like so many other analysts, pays inadequate attention to Puškin's many remarks about good noblemen and good commanders. Puškin clearly discriminates between those Russian military leaders of high and low rank, who take timely, resolute, and courageous action against the rebel forces, and those who vacillate, wait timidly ensconced behind fortress walls, or abandon their troops altogether to seek refuge away from the field of battle.

Puškin describes the futile early efforts made by the Russian government against the growing menace in the southeast corner of the Empire. In his judgment, the main reason for these failures was the gross ineptitude and cowardice of Catherine's military commanders such as Černyšev, Rejnsdorp, and Kar. Kar's nerves shattered completely under duress, he feigned illness to escape personal danger, was drummed out of the service, and lived out his life in ignominy on a private estate.

No progress was made in stemming the tide of insurrection until Catherine chose General Bibikov to command her forces in the battle area. A summary of the latter's outstanding earlier triumphs in the Seven Years' War, in civil counter-insurgency, and in civic affairs is prefixed by Puškin's remark that "Aleksandr Il'ič Bibikov belongs among the most remarkable persons of Catherine's times, which were so rich in eminent people." (IX, 32.) The historian also points out that while Bibikov's career of public service had earned him the Empress' favor, Catherine disliked his tendency to complain and express candidly his own critical opinions. Puškin writes:

> Bibikov was coldly received by the Empress, who heretofore had always been friendly to him. Perhaps she was displeased with the indiscreet words which he had been compelled to utter from vexation;[16] for while ardent in action and devoted heart and soul to Her Majesty, Bibikov was a grumbler and bold in his judgments. (IX, 32.)

Nevertheless, according to this account, Catherine had seen the necessity for strong measures against the burgeoning evil of rebellion, kept her prejudices in check, and dispatched the irascible but proven field commander to the front. Bibikov emerges as one of the authentic heroes of the war and is warmly eulogized by Puškin with the following words:

> Deržavin celebrated the demise of Bibikov in verse. Catherine mourned for him and showered his family with her generosities. Petersburg and Moscow were struck with horror. Soon all of Russia as well sensed an irrevocable loss. (IX, 54.)

After Bibikov's death, there was an urgent need for another such brave and sagacious Commander-in-Chief. For in the summer of 1774 there began the second, and more dangerous phase of the struggle, when Pugačev's armies were ravaging the west bank of the Volga and attracting thousands of Russian peasant serfs to their ranks. The eminent Princes Ščerbatov and Golicyn had failed to provide effective overall direction to the campaign. For a moment, Catherine considered taking charge of the troops herself. But, at the crucial time, she and the Empire were again rescued by an old and faithful public servant, Count Petr Ivanovič Panin. Puškin writes:

At that time a famous dignitary [*vel'moža*], who had been removed from the court and, like Bibikov, was in disfavor, Count Petr Ivanovič Panin, offered to take upon himself the great task, which had not been completed by his predecessor. Catherine observed with gratitude the ardor of her noble subject, and Count Panin, just when he, having armed his own peasants and domestic servants was preparing to move against Pugačev, received in his village the order to assume command over those provinces where the revolt was raging, and over the troops which had been sent there. (IX, 69-70.)

The excellent coordination of Russian military units during the final months of the campaign implies that, in Puškin's view, Count Panin brought order and resourcefulness to the command.[17]

The real hero of Puškin's account is one of the lesser field grade officers whose exploits were appreciated both by Bibikov and by Panin. Puškin gives extremely high praise to Lieutenant Colonel Ivan Ivanovič Mixel'son, the Russified German commander whose relentless pursuit of Pugačev's main force throughout the year 1774 finally resulted in the defeat of the insurrection and the capture of its leader. He attempts to rescue the military reputation of Mixel'son, who in July 1774 liberated Kazan' and who, Puškin believed, had been erroneously maligned in previous accounts of the battle. Puškin writes:

History must refute the slander which has been thoughtlessly repeated in society; it has been affirmed that Mixel'son could have prevented the taking of Kazan', but that he deliberately gave the rebels time to pillage the city, in order to profit in turn from the rich booty, preferring any sort of gain to the glory, honors, and royal decorations which awaited the saviour of Kazan' and suppressor of the revolt! The readers have seen how quickly and how indefatigably Mixel'son pursued Pugačev. If Potemkin and Brant had done their work and succeeded in holding out just a few hours, then Kazan' would have been saved. Mixel'son's soldiers, of course, enriched themselves, but it would be shameful for us to blame unjustly an old, distinguished warrior, who spent his whole life on the field of honor and died as Commander-in-Chief of the Russian armies. (IX, 67.)[18]

In summary, the Russian governments of the eighteenth century are shown in *A History of Pugačev* to have brought upon themselves the consternation and resentment of the Yaik Cossacks by their abrupt, callous, and largely unnecessary attempt to force that border people and its homeland into an alien political and administrative mold. Venal and arbitrary Russian officials sent into the region to enforce a new regime even exceeded and abused their authority, thus intensifying Cossack animosity until the whole area rose up in rebellion.

The Russian administrative and military apparatus in contiguous regions, such as Orenburg and Kazan', was at that time in the hands of inept and cowardly officials. When the Yaik Cossack rebellion quickly spread into their midst, the response of these officials was timid, disorganized, and almost totally inadequate. Moreover, the fact that supposedly loyal Cossacks and many other government soldiers defected to the rebel enemy and that the ranks of the insurgency swelled with the addition of Kalmyks, Bashkirs, Tartars, Chuvash, and Mordvinians, and Russian runaway and liberated slave laborers, indicates how close the Russian Empire had been, at least at its fringes, to the kindling point. Popular resentment of Russian rule had by no means been limited to the Yaik region alone.

At first, even the military units dispatched from the center were unable to cope with the expertly led and popularly supported uprising. Once again poor leadership was the main reason.[19]

Finally, and most importantly, in the summer of 1774 when Pugačev's army crossed the Volga into Russia proper, they proved that there too was a situation ripe for revolt.

> Pugačev was fleeing; but his flight seemed like an invasion. Never had his successes been more terrifying, never had the rebellion raged with such force. Insurrection spread from one village to another, from province to province. The mere arrival of two or three villains was sufficient to arouse whole regions. Separate bands of pillagers and rebels were organized; and each one had its own Pugačev. (IX, 69.)

In the early stages of the rebellion, after each capture of a fort along the Yaik River, a few public executions were ordered by Pugačev. The rebels usually hanged the commandant and one or more of his lieutenants. There were even cases of an officer's life being spared, especially if the common people or the garrison soldiers testified that he had been fair to them. However, in the second phase of the war, on the west bank of the Volga, it was not only local chieftains who had to fear for their lives, but also the landed gentry. In Puškin's words:

> The province chiefs fled from their cities, the noblemen from their estates; the rabble caught them both in flight and delivered them from everywhere to Pugačev. (IX, 68.)

The implication is clear. The common townspeople and peasant serfs of eastern Russia chose to cast their lot with all manner of non-Russian riff-raff from beyond the Volga rather than to stand beside their masters to preserve the empire and the feudal system of land tenure and serfdom to which they had been bound. The dispossessed and downtrodden of Kurmyš, Saransk, Penza, and elsewhere in Russia instinctively felt more in common with rebellious Cossacks, Bashkirs, and the like than with their beardless, Europeanized aristocratic compatriots who had preached enlightenment while treating their serfs as less than men.

The Russian empire, in Puškin's view, was saved from ruin only when Catherine, as a last resort, relieved her favorites Ščerbatov and Golicyn and turned to noblemen of an older, different stripe. It is more than a coincidence that Bibikov, the hero of 1773 until he died, and Panin, the finally victorious Commander-in-Chief, had both been in Imperial disfavor until called upon to lead in a time of extreme danger.

One passing reference to Count Panin suggests that there also existed a more benevolent and more beloved kind of gentry landowner than those who had been forced to flee their estates or be hanged by their serfs at the first opportunity. We are told that Panin, when he received the order to assume overall command of the rebellious provinces, "having armed his own peasants and domestic servants, was preparing to move against Pugačev" (IX, 70.) A nobleman would hardly be inclined to arm his men unless their loyalty to him was assured.

It is implied that leaders such as Panin and Bibikov were available but that their efforts were utilized and appreciated only in a dire emergency. Puškin writes that it was jealousy on the part of Rumjancev, one of Catherine's favorites, toward Bibikov, which delayed the dispatch of Suvorov to the embattled areas. The great hero of foreign campaigns arrived on the scene only on the eve of Pugačev's capture and in time to interrogate personally the rebel leader in the village of Yaik, cradle of the now defeated rebellion.

As is usually the case with Puškin's writings in any mode or genre, there is more in *A History of Pugačev* than initially meets the eye. There is more than his own tongue-in-cheek description of the work as a straightforward account of "military operations until then virtually unknown"; there is more than a compilation of interesting documents and a symptom of the repentant nobleman complex, as Raeff has suggested; there is more than a model of felicitous historiographical prose, and there is more than the documentary underpinning for a subsequent historical novel.

The most significant aspect of *A History of Pugačev,* at least for the student of Russian literature and cultural history, is its polemical basis, the implicit point-of-view from which it was written. As might be expected, Puškin presents in this treatise an interpretation of the historical events which is bold, idiosyncratic, revisionist. Its main elements are as follows: (1) before Peter the Great, the Yaik (Ural) Cossacks were a free, independent, and largely autonomous people living in one of Muscovy's border regions, in relative tranquility, according to their native traditions; (2) Russian imperial policies of the eighteenth century tended to alienate and disorient large segments of the Yaik Cossack population by forcing them into conformity with laws, tax assessments, forms of land tenure, and state service which encroached upon their indigenous economy, political organization, customs, and mores; (3) during the reign of

Catherine the Great, the Yaik Cossacks were finally goaded into rebellion by the Russian government; (4) Pugačev, himself a Don Cossack, appeared at an opportune moment and was singled out almost at once as the leader of the movement; (5) the insurrection quickly spread to the oppressed factory serfs of the Urals, to the Bashkirs, to other non-Russian, non-Orthodox native people, and ultimately, to the Russian serf population which was itself vulnerable to incitation; (6) Pugačev's armies most everywhere were met with open arms by all classes and groupings, save the Russian landed aristocracy and local imperial administration; (7) the Russian military apparatus (especially in the level of high command) was woefully ill-prepared for a civic emergency of such huge proportions; (8) for a time, there was a danger that Moscow would be captured by the rebels and that the Russian Empire would collapse; (9) the situation was rescued, the rebellion defeated, and order restored, only after Catherine II replaced her originally-chosen, but inept, military leaders, with distinguished gentlemen who were previously in disgrace, but had long since proven their mettle not only in combat, but in public service and private endeavors (that is, as benevolent but efficient serf holders).

In this, the first, serious attempt at a history of the Pugačev rebellion, Puškin's sympathies lay at once with the Cossacks who had been intimidated by the central government, and with those representatives of the Russian *narod* who had been treated cruelly by their gentry masters. There is even an element of admiration, however grudging, for Pugačev himself in Puškin's work. For however crude, vengeful, and recklessly visionary the rebel leader may have been, he was (in Puškin's eyes) a brilliant military strategist and a gifted natural leader of men. Puškin waits, of course, until his novel *The Captain's Daughter* to suggest that Pugačev may also have been a warm, perceptive, and understanding, though certainly unpredictable, human being on a personal level, perhaps in some sense an amalgam of many traits, both laudable and reprehensible, of the Russian national character. The real heroes of *A History of Pugačev,* however, are the "good" noblemen — Bibikov, Panin, and Mixel'son — who, when summoned out of retirement or public obscurity, respond to the call of duty by taking charge of the Russian armies, by reversing the fortunes of war in favor of the government, and, ultimately, by bringing Pugačev and his rebellion to their knees. This is Puškin's way of saying, under the very eye of the censor and of Nicholas I, that the latter's grandmother had too long relied upon the wrong people and had pursued a policy of keeping the true patriots and aristocrats away from the levers of state. And Puškin's view of the Pugačev rebellion fits in entirely with his decade-long campaign (1826-1837) to persuade Nicholas I to restore the rights and the influence of the old, hereditary, "enlightened" nobility (*prosveščennoe dvorjanstvo*) which he perceived to have been disenfranchised, impoverished, and rendered socially and politically impotent during the eighteenth and early nineteenth century.

Considering his many disadvantages, it is perfectly understandable that Puškin, writing in 1833, did not pronounce the final word or compose a definitive treatise on the Pugačev affair. After all, Russian historiography was still in an early stage of its development; many key documents were not made available to Puškin for his research (most notably, the so-called "Sledstvennoe delo o Pugačeve,"[20] the official transcript of the interrogation of the captured Pugačev and the record of the government investigation into the affair; Puškin was an untrained and as yet inexperienced historian; and finally, he was breaking new ground by writing about a previously forbidden topic, one so sensitive and controversial that it took considerable courage even to discuss it in polite society. Considering these impediments, it is certainly to Puškin's credit that his *History of Pugačev* can be faulted so seldom for factual errors and retains its lively interest quite apart from the overall literary reputation of its author. And while the main purpose of the Puškin scholar is to determine the place of this work in Puškin's *oeuvre* as a whole, and to indicate in what ways it reflects his particular *Weltanschauung,* rather than to evaluate its worth in relation to Pugačev scholarship 150 years later, one can only marvel at *A History of Pugačev* for the succinctness and expressiveness of its style, for the vividness and dramatic force of its descriptions of events, for its memorableness in bringing to life a host of historical characters, and for the shrewdness of its insights into the causes, dimensions, consequences, and lessons of the Pugačev rebellion.

Puškin's ultimate reasons for writing *A History of Pugačev* may have been literary in character. The entire, painstaking historiographical project may have remained in its intent closely linked to the projected historical novel about the times of Pugačev. And *The Captain's Daughter* may overshadow *A History of Pugačev* for another 150 years or longer as a source of images and information about this crucial period in Russian history. After all, the touching story of Maša Mironova, Petr Andreevič Grinev, and their relationship to Pugačev personally and to his times, occupies a deservedly hallowed place in both Russian and world literature. Nevertheless, *A History of Pugačev* withstands scrutiny according to its own lights. It represents a significant event in Russian historiography and retains its interest today not only because it was written by Puškin but because of its merits as a work of historical scholarship. He went to considerable pains to obtain all the relevant sources, both published and unpublished, and with care and thoroughness collated, cross-checked, and critically evaluated these sources before accepting anything as fact or as significant historical detail. Despite numerous handicaps, Puškin observed in practice during his years of field work[21] and archival toil high standards of scholarly conscience in his methodology and produced, in *A History of Pugačev,* work of considerable value.

In creating this work, Puškin thus accomplished a number of closely interrelated purposes. He rescued from government-imposed oblivion the memory of Pugačev; he placed before Russian society hundreds of fascinating documents and a concise account of events relating to one of the most crucial turning points in Russia's history; he forced his contemporaries to consider the implications of this nearly-catastrophic war; he helped us to understand better than before his own views on the Russian nobility and on the Russian nation in the 1770's; and he mentioned a historical prototype, however atypical, for a new theme which he would develop fully on a symbolic level in *The Captain's Daughter* — the theme of alliance between insurgent Cossacks and peasants, on the one hand, and dissident noblemen, on the other. To be sure, Puškin diversified his palette as an all-round man of letters with the writing of *A History of Pugačev*. And later, in weaving historical details into a fictional romantic story, he showed how closely erudition is linked to artistic talent in the creative process leading to an entertaining, informative, and enduring literary masterpiece. But it is also clear from a close reading of *A History of Pugačev* that Puškin — with his passion for significant detail, his rigorous intellectual honesty, and his inimitable literary gifts — successfully achieved for himself an independent scholarly reputation and identity — that of the *littérateur* as historian.

NOTES

1. Thus, topics like "Puškin's historical views," "Puškin the historian," and "history in the works of Puškin" have become legitimate and even popular scholarly aspects through which to view the author's genius. The scholarship on these topics available in Russian to 1966 is summarized in V. V. Pugačev, "Istoričeskaja proza," *Puškin: itogi i problemy izučenija* (Moscow, Leningrad: Nauka, 1966), 502-13. A more complete bibliography of secondary sources on Puškin and history (in Russian and English) can be found in my unpublished doctoral dissertation entitled "Pushkin and the History of the Russian Nobility" (University of Wisconsin, 1971; also available through University Microfilms).

2. See, for example, A. V. Predtečenskij, "Istoričeskie vzgljady A. S. Puškina," *Očerki istorii istoričeskoi nauki v S.S.S.R.,* I (Moscow: Nauka, 1955), 304-10, and, for a Western view, Michael Karpovich, "Pushkin as an Historian," *Centennial Essays for Pushkin* (Cambridge, Mass.: Harvard University Press, 1937), 181-200.

3. The extent to which Puškin's "Materials for a *History of Peter I*" appear to be finished (at least in places) is documented in I. L. Fejnberg, *Nezaveršennye raboty Puškina* (Moscow, 1958; 4-oe izd., 1964).

4. Originally entitled *A History of the Pugačev Revolt (Istorija pugačevskogo bunta).* Nicholas I himself changed the title, offering the explanation that "a criminal like Pugačev does not have [deserve] his own history."

In recent years Soviet historians and literary scholars have made enormous strides in the elucidation of Puškin's sources, methodology, and the publication circumstances which resulted in this remarkable book. The most important work in this area has been done by Redžinal'd Ovčinnikov in his candidate's dissertation of 1965, later published in part as *Puškin at Work on Archival Documents: A History of Pugačev [Puškin v rabote nad arxivnymi dokumentami: "Istorija Pugačeva"]* (Leningrad: Nauka, 1969). Citations from this book are given in text and in notes in parentheses, e.g., (Ovč., 34.). Puškin the historian, while maintaining a high standard of thoroughness and objectivity, does not by any means lose his way in the maelstrom of often conflicting documentary testimony. Ovčinnikov shows that Puškin "utilized critically all available historical sources... [and] strove for maximum authenticity in the portrayal of events." (Ovč., 150.) Despite the great deal of attention given to military operations, Puškin does not overencumber his narrative with tactical details. "The description of events is so generalized that it seems to break away from concrete particulars while at the same time reconstructing an integrated historical picture." (Ovč., 137.)

5. One suspects that not only his means of expression but also the very choice of content was governed largely by Puškin's esthetic instincts. "He selected documents and facts which would portray the essence of described events in the boldest relief, in the most picturesque and moving way [*naibolee relefno, koloritno i èmotsional'no*]." (Ovč., 150.)

6. Puškin's reliance upon his own historical research as preparation for the eventual attainment of a novelistic goal was observed by several Soviet scholars preceeding Ovčinnikov. Julian Oksman, for example, once referred to *A History of Pugačev* as a "wide screen [to be used] for the detailed illumination of the basic chapters of the novel [*The Captain's Daughter*]," in his introductory article "Puškin v rabote nad romanom *Kapitanskaja dočka,*" (Moscow: Nauka, 1964), 208. I too have attempted to show that Puškin's ultimate literary purposes with the Pugačev theme were realized only in *The Captain's Daughter,* where he developed on a symbolic level a notion which was present only potentially and inconspicuously in the historical monograph – the dream of an alliance between insurgent Cossacks and peasants, on the one hand, and dissident noblemen, on the other. See Gerald

E. Mikkelson, "The Mythopoetic Element in Pushkin's Historical Novel *The Captain's Daughter,*" *Canadian-American Slavic Studies* (Fall 1973), 296-313.

7. Two of the most stimulating expressions of preference for *The Captain's Daughter* over *A History of Pugačev* are found in V. O. Ključevskij, "Značenie Puškina dlja russkoj istoriografii," *A. S. Puškin v ego značenii xudožestvennom, istoričeskom i obščestvennom* (Moscow, 1905), 168 [see Ključcevskij, *Sočinenija,* VII (Moscow, 1959), 145-51]; and Marina Cvetaeva, "Puškin i Pugačev," *Voprosy literatury,* No. 8 (1965), 174-95 [reprinted in Marina Cvetaeva, *Moj Puškin* (Moscow, 1967)].

8. In Puškin's letter to Count Benkendorf of December 6, 1833, in which he requests the Emperor's permission to publish *Istorija Pugačeva;* A. S. Puškin, *Polnoe sobranie sočinenij v 17-i tomax* (Moscow, Leningrad: AN SSSR, 1937-59), XV, 98. All quotations from the writings of Puškin will be drawn from this "large" Academy edition. They will be cited in text in parentheses by volume number (Roman numerals) and page numbers (Arabic).

9. *Istorija pugačevskogo bunta* was published in late 1834 upon the personal authorization of Nicholas I and without the usual obstacles of formal censorship, an event entirely without precedent in Puškin's literary career. A recent study suggests that Puškin's revisionist interpretation of the Pugačev uprising fitted into the Emperor's political plans at the time in relation to the nobility. See N. N. Petrunina, "Kak uvidela svet *Istorija Pugačeva,*" in the book *Nad stranicami Puškina* (Leningrad: Nauka, 1974), 124-37.

10. Marc Raeff and John T. Alexander, two of the leading U.S. specialists on eighteenth-century Russia, both acknowledge the importance of Puškin's contribution as the first historian of the Pugačev Rebellion and the first publisher of numerous valuable documents included and appended to his work. Cf. Marc Raeff, "Pugachev's Rebellion," *Preconditions of Revolution in Early Modern Europe,* ed. Robert Forster and Jack P. Greene (Baltimore and London, 1970), 161-202, and John T. Alexander, *Emperor of the Cossacks: Pugachev and the Frontier Jacquerie of 1773-1775* (Lawrence, KS: Coronado Press, 1973), 195. Moreover, these recent studies tend to corroborate, rather than refute, Puškin's contentions regarding the causes of the rebellion. Therefore, it is quite inexplicable to me why Raeff does not give higher marks to Puškin's *A History of Pugačev* as historiography. Raeff finds it "by today's standards and taste. . . pretty boring,. . . what L. Febvre's school derides as *histoire évenementielle* ["a history of events," G. E. M.] (Raeff, 200). Alexander emphatically disagrees, as do the leading Soviet specialists, e.g., V. V. Mavrodin and A. I. Andruščenko.

11. It is nothing new to point out that Puškin interpreted the great civil insurrection of 1773-74 in terms of social classes, or estates — as a revolt of the oppressed against their despotic masters. Soviet historians and Puškinists have been particularly inclined to stress this point. However, they fall into error when trying to make Puškin into their own kind of champion of the people.

12. Puškin paraphrased the last two sentences of this statement in his *Istorija Pugačeva* (IX, 45) and published the entire letter in an appendix (IX, 201-2).

13. In the same letter Puškin indicated that as a historian of the Pugačev affair his conscience was far from satisfied. He requested permission to read the account of the government's interrogation of Pugačev, one of the most important documents which had not been at his disposal in 1833 and 1834 (see XVI, 7-8). In February 1835 the Pugačev dossier was transferred to the State Archive for Puškin's use.

14. Švanvič served as a prototype for the traitor Švabrin in Puškin's historical novel *The Captain's Daughter.*

15. V. V. Mavrodin, *Krestjanskaja vojna v Rossii v 1773-1775: Vosstanie Pugačeva,* I (Leningrad, 1961), 37.

16. Bibikov had recently been relieved as Commander-in-Chief of Russian armies in Poland, an assignment which he had executed with the utmost distinction and which had even earned him the love and trust of the vanquished Poles.

17. Once again, Puškin appended a note to his narrative in which Panin's public career is summarized in approving terms (IX, 116).

18. A footnote to this paragraph (IX, 115) gives further praise to the character and bravery of Mixel'son, and he is even singled out for his decisive role in the defeat of Pugačev by being mentioned in Puškin's historical novel *The Captain's Daughter*. Near the end of Chapter 13, just prior to describing his own arrest, Grinev junior remarks that "Pugačev was in flight and being pursued by Ivan Ivanovič Mixel'son. We soon heard of his complete defeat." (VIII, 364.) The same words are found at the end of the "Omitted Chapter" (VIII, 384).

19. "Analyzing the measures taken by Pugačev and his collaborators, one must admit that the rebels chose the means which were most promising and most conducive to the achievement of their goal. The government for its part acted weakly, slowly, erratically." From Puškin's "General Remarks" on the conflict. (IX, 375-76.)

20. Only on February 26, 1835, after *A History of Pugačev* was published, Puškin received permission to utilize this document. He continued to study its contents until the end of August 1835.

21. With the government's permission, in 1833 Puškin visited Kazan' and Orenburg for a personal inspection of the areas where the Pugačev uprising had taken place and for interviews with some of the few remaining eyewitnesses.

PUŠKIN AND BELINSKIJ: THE ROLE OF THE "OFFENDED PROVINCIAL"

George Gutsche, Northern Illinois University

The persona-author is one of the most interesting devices Puškin used in his journalism. By using such a device — a fictional character with an independent personality — Puškin could accomplish tasks which would have been difficult to achieve had he written under his real name, with a pseudonym, or simply anonymously. The persona-author was a device Puškin employed on three occasions in his journalism, twice in articles by "Feofilakt Kosičkin" that appeared in 1831 in *The Telescope* (*Teleskop*), and once in an article that appeared in 1836 in Puškin's own journal, *The Contemporary* (*Sovremennik*).[1] In the earlier articles, which were directed against the minor novelist and police spy Faddej Bulgarin, the identity of Puškin's persona had been relatively transparent; the identity of his 1836 persona, however, was such a carefully kept secret it did not become generally known until the 1920's.[2] The reasons why Puškin chose to conceal his identity behind a persona, as well as the functions that this persona helped fulfill, may be found within the journalistic context of the day and, in particular, within the fabric of his relationship with two other notable figures of Russian letters, Gogol' and Belinskij.[3]

Although there is a substantial body of data and scholarly material relating to Puškin and Gogol',[4] the available evidence on Puškin's relationship with Belinskij is slight and susceptible to a variety of interpretations. The references Puškin has his persona make to Belinskij represent a crucial piece of evidence that is frequently adduced to support the claim that Puškin's interest in having the young critic (Belinskij was then 25 years old) write for his journal had positive ideological implications with respect to Puškin's development. What Puškin's persona says about Belinskij in *The Contemporary*, however, is both positive and critical.[5] In an effort to find an ideological kinship between Puškin and Belinskij, previous scholarship has not given enough attention to the possibility that Puškin, through his persona A. B., was instructing or educating both Belinskij and Gogol' about his role as editor, and was not necessarily making any significant ideological commitment to Belinskij. An analysis of the function and character of Puškin's persona in *The Contemporary* will provide a framework through which we can assess the fascinating and problematic issue of Puškin's relationship with Belinskij.

The appearance of Puškin's persona in *The Contemporary* was preceded by the following series of events. For the first issue of the journal in 1836 Gogol' wrote a major review of the leading periodicals of the day. This review, entitled "On the Trend of Journal Literature," was understood by readers and journalists working for other periodicals as a statement of *The Contemporary*'s program, as an expression of Puškin's aims for his new journal; Gogol''s review was understood in this way principally because it appeared anonymously.[6] Since there was nothing else in the issue that might be construed as an editorial statement or program, the public reasonably assumed that Gogol''s essay constituted the journal's program. For the third issue of *The Contemporary* of that year Puškin composed and had printed a "letter to the publisher"; the author of this letter was identified only as "A. B." from Tver'.[7] In the letter, Puškin's persona discussed Gogol''s provocative review and referred to it as the program of *The Contemporary*. This reference of A. B. to the journal's program gave Puškin the opportunity to deny tactfully, in an editorial note, that the review article was in any sense programmatic. Puškin's editorial note will be cited in full below.

By using a note and his persona's letter Puškin could thus disavow Gogol''s essay, and even criticize it without offending the psychologically fragile Gogol' and without giving the impression that there were internal problems relating to the direction of the new journal. The persona's letter served yet another function by making reference to Belinskij, whose name had not been mentioned in Gogol''s survey:[8]

> "I regret that you didn't mention Mr. Belinskij in speaking about *The Telescope*. He shows talent which offers great hope. If to independence of opinion and his wit he unites more scholarship, more knowledge of books, more respect for tradition, more prudence — in a word, more maturity — we would have an extremely remarkable critic." (210)

What makes A. B.'s letter especially interesting is this characterization of the young critic, but what complicates interpretation is the fact that Puškin describes Belinskij through a persona whose views need not necessarily reflect his own. Moreover, if the characterization of Belinskij is positive, it is also very cautious and qualified. A. B.'s remarks have been taken to reveal something of Puškin's attitude toward Belinskij, and have usually been considered in conjunction with letters indicating that Puškin, in the summer and late fall of 1836, took steps in the direction of inviting Belinskij, who was then writing for *The Telescope,* to join *The Contemporary.* The plan was never realized. Belinskij's difficulties resulting from the publication of Čaadaev's controversial letter in *The Telescope,* and Puškin's well known personal problems at the end of 1836 may explain why negotiations between the two were broken off. It was not until 1847, ten years after Puškin's death, that Belinskij came to *The Contemporary,* then under the editorship of Nekrasov and Panaev.

Puškin's desire to have Belinskij write for *The Contemporary* is suggested in two letters, one written in late May from Puškin to his personal friend and assistant with the journal, P. V. Naščokin, and one written at the end of October or the beginning of November from Naščokin to Puškin. The relevant section of the first letter reads:

". . . Now let's talk about business. I left you two extra copies of *The Contemporary*. Give one to Prince Gagarin, and send the other from me to Belinskij (N. B.: but keep it secret from the Observers), and have him told that I regret very much that I didn't succeed in seeing him. . . ."[9]

From this letter it is apparent that Puškin attempted to meet Belinskij in Moscow in May of 1836, and from the later letter to Puškin we learn that Naščokin made inquiries about Belinskij's willingness to work for Puškin.[10] What can be said beyond all this is largely speculative. Pogodin recalled in his memoirs some time later (1869) that Puškin was initially attracted by Belinskij's "Literary Reveries" ("Literaturnye mečtanija"), which appeared in 1834, and that he saw in Belinskij an influential and brilliant polemicist.[11] The fact that copies of *The Telescope* in Puškin's personal library were cut only for Belinskij's writings strongly supports the contention that Puškin followed Belinskij's career rather closely in 1835 and 1836.[12]

Why Puškin should wish to keep secret his personal "gift" to Belinskij may be explained by reference to the journalistic situation of the day. In reviews throughout 1835 and 1836 Belinskij often criticized, using the pejorative terms *svetskost'* and *aristokratizm*, the overly refined, superficial, and snobbish opinions of *The Moscow Observer* (whose editors and associates Puškin called "Observers" in his correspondence).[13] Public knowledge of plans for an alliance between Puškin and their severest critic and polemical opponent might jeopardize the relationship Puškin had with this group. His letters to his wife from Moscow in May of 1836 suggest that he thought it was important for the success of *The Contemporary* that he maintain amicable relations with the "Observers."[14] Perceiving that they were already somewhat cool toward him and his new enterprise in St. Petersburg, and yet apparently desirous of having avenues open for possible contributions and allies in Moscow, Puškin understandably showed concern about needlessly provoking them.

Ironically, while Puškin throughout 1836 was quietly laying the groundwork for inviting Belinskij to join him, his two close associates and assistants with the second issue of *The Contemporary* — Kraevskij and Odoevskij — were, for their own reasons, plotting with the "Observers" (behind Puškin's back) for the establishment of a new journal.[15]

In this very complicated and surely frustrating situation, Puškin was badly in need of allies. To make matters worse, the article by Gogol', which was understood by the public as the new program of *The Contemporary,* adopted an antagonistic stance against the most widely read journal of the time, *The Library for Reading* (*Biblioteka čtenija*), edited by the Polish émigré-scholar O..I. Senkovskij.

Gogol''s article had dealt briefly and not too kindly with *The Moscow Observer,* despite the fact that his friends Pogodin and Ševyrev were closely associated with it. His basic criticism – and this accusation he leveled at most journals of the time – was that *The Moscow Observer* did not criticize *The Library* strongly enough. Because Gogol''s article, which appeared anonymously, was generally understood as setting the tone of Puškin's new journal, opposition to *The Library* was assumed to be an essential component of the program of *The Contemporary*. Puškin's persona notes this at the beginning of his letter:

> "The essay 'On the Trend of Journal Literature' justly attracted general attention. In it you wittily, cuttingly, and straightforwardly set forth very many just observations. But I confess that it does not correspond to what we expected from the trend that you were going to give your criticism. Reading through this somewhat inconsistent essay carefully, the thing that I saw most clearly was great bitterness toward Mr. Senkovskij. In your opinion our entire literature revolves around *The Library for Reading*. All other periodical publications were examined only in relation to it." (206-07)

Much of the persona's letter dealt with Gogol''s accusations about *The Library*. These accusations mostly concerned the journal's editorial policies and the editor's capabilities as a critic. That the refutation of specific charges against *The Library* was expressed by someone from the provinces had special significance, for *The Library* was apparently designed to appeal to readers in the provinces. Under the editorship of Senkovskij *The Library* had become an enormously successful periodical with a variety of departments and a readership far surpassing that of other journals. Belinskij attributed much of this success to the fact that *The Library* was a provincial journal. In a long article of seven installments he explained the journal's popular success by reference to its editor's skill, cleverness, punctuality, and practical abilities; the main reason for its success, however, was that it was designed for and answered the needs of a provincial readership. Implicit in Belinskij's account was disdain for the taste and intelligence of readers in the provinces. Gogol' showed to some extent a similar attitude in his essay.[16] It could hardly be an accident that Puškin chose to make the author of his letter to the editor an offended provincial; the letter could then serve as a refutation of the specific charges of Belinskij and Gogol' by exemplifying the wit, understanding, judgment, and intelligence of a provincial. The following discussion of the letter's principal features should shed some light on Puškin's relationship with other journals and journalists of the time, including Belinskij.

A. B.'s letter, including Puškin's editorial response, was relatively long, almost 1500 words. The letter covered a variety of topics and gave ample evidence of the persona's distinct personality. He begins with a reference to a moral principle extracted from a sermon of Georgij Koniskij, a Belorussian bishop whose writing Puškin had favorably reviewed in the first issue of *The*

Contemporary: teachers have an obligation to heed their own words before preaching to others. Since Puškin made no reference to this principle in his review, we are to assume that A. B. himself read Koniskij's works — an accomplishment which is presumably a credit to provincials. Turning this principle on Gogol''s essay, A. B. points out that the essay contained criticism of other journals of the day for lacking a definite goal, but offered no such goal for *The Contemporary.* In the main A. B.'s criticism of Gogol''s essay focuses on inconsistencies.

Throughout the letter, A. B. gives the impression of impartiality and moderation by balancing praise with criticism, avoiding as far as possible a polemical tone. For example, in the lines cited earlier, he first praised Gogol''s piece for its style and then became more critical, pointing out its bitterness toward *The Library.* Gogol' had not said that the goal of *The Contemporary* was to criticize *The Library,* but this is apparently the interpretation the public gave the essay, with some assistance from Senkovskij who was expecting such a goal.[17]

A. B. first lists, in summary fashion, Gogol''s accusations against *The Library* (just as Kosičkin had done in his battle with Bulgarin), and then analyzes each one:

"1. Mr. Senkovskij took exclusive control over the critical section of the journal published in the name of the bookseller Smirdin.
2. Mr. Senkovskij corrects essays which he receives for publication in *The Library.*
3. In his critical judgments Mr. Senkovskij does not always observe a tone of seriousness and dispassionateness.
4. Mr. Senkovskij does not use the pronouns *sej* and *onyj.*
5. Mr. Senkovskij has about five thousand subscribers." (207)

Gogol' had shown considerable concern for *The Library*'s monopolistic power and Senkovskij's domination of the journal's tone ("From the publication of the first book, the public saw that in the journal reigned the tone, opinions, and thoughts of one person. . .") and had also stressed the fact that Senkovskij, in his habit of "correcting" works submitted to him for publication had even put his own ending on Fonvizin's *The Minor.*

A. B. relegates the first two points to the "domestic, so to speak, arrangements of the bookseller Smirdin" which "do not concern the public."[18] The virtue of this move is in its subtlety: A. B. does not attempt to disprove the charges that Senkovskij is a virtual dictator in his journal's policies and that he has the presumption to "correct" the work of others, but simply says that these points are not relevant to the reading public. It was, however, primarily upon these points that Gogol' wrote. The effect of A. B.'s first mentioning the points and then explicitly refusing to comment on them is that of reinforcement through repetition. Even though these two points may truly be irrelevant to public concern, they are not irrelevant to prospective contributors to journals.

In reference to the third issue — maintaining the proper tone in reviews — A. B. first advances the principle that works should be judged with a tone appropriate to their quality, and then turns Gogol''s argument against him by pointing out that in the same issue of *The Contemporary* in which his essay appeared, Gogol' had used a tone far from serious in describing a new periodical of the day:

> "And allow me to inquire: What is the meaning of your critique of the almanac *My New Home* (*Moe novosel'e*), which you so felicitously compared to a scrawny cat miaowing on the roof of the emptied house? A very amusing comparison, but I don't see anything serious in it. Physician! Heal thyself! I confess, some of the funny critiques which have dotted *The Library for Reading* pleased me unutterably, and I would have been very sorry if the critic had preferred to maintain a majestic silence." (208)

The fourth issue relates to the controversy then over the use of the pronouns *sej* and *onyj*. Senkovskij believed that since these words were no longer used in conversation in polite society they had no place in the literary language.[19] On this particular point Belinskij tended to agree with Senkovskij, for he too avoided them and on occasion even made fun of them. A. B., however, appears not to have taken the controversy seriously: "Mr. Senkovskij's jokes about the innocent pronouns *sej, sija, sie, onyj, onaja, onoe* are nothing but jokes." This line, it turns out, is only the introduction to A. B.'s serious reservations about Senkovskij's views:

> "The public, and even a few writers, were free to take them [the pronouns] as the real thing. Can the written language be exactly like the spoken one? No, just as the spoken language can never be exactly like the written one. Not just the pronouns *sej* and *onyj*, but the participle in general and a multitude of essential words are usually avoided in conversation. . . . But it does not follow from this that the participle should be expunged from the Russian language. The richer the language is in expressions and turns of phrase, the better it is for a clever writer. The written language is constantly animated by expressions born in conversation, but it should not renounce what it has invented in the course of centuries. Writing solely the spoken language means not knowing the language." (208-09)

A great deal was accomplished by A. B. in these lines. Not only did he manage to toss some sharp barbs at Senkovskij (and his knowledge of Russian), but he also was able to demonstrate, by means of rational argument, the logical and literary sophistication of provincials. The linguistic argument A. B. boldly offers here serves as a contrast to the pompously expressed linguistic idealism of Senkovskij.

What is also of interest here is A. B.'s subtle strategic shift in approach. It seemed at first that A. B. intended to defend Senkovskij against what he thought were unjustified attacks by Gogol'. But instead of defending the fourth point, *viz.*, that Senkovskij did not use the pronouns in question, A. B. refers to Senkovskij's efforts to justify his position as "jokes." If they were only jokes, however, what purpose is served by discussing them? A. B. apparently does not really regard them as jokes, for he offers a convincing counter-argument to Senkovskij's claims. Thus A. B. is now in the position of attacking him in arguments which are considerably more substantial and persuasive than those of Gogol'. After offering the kind of argument that Gogol' should have presented, A. B., in a brilliant stroke of irony, ends the paragraph with the pronoun *onyj*.

A. B.'s comments on the fifth issue, concerning the number of subscribers to *The Library,* need no discussion: "As for the fifth point, i.e., the 5,000 subscribers, allow me to express the sincere wish that next year you can deserve precisely the same accusation."

Further remarks characterize positively Senkovskij's work as editor (for example, his industry and punctuality), but A. B.'s final two sentences on Senkovskij conceal a subtle criticism:

> "We humble provincials are grateful to him — for the variety of his essays, for the thickness of the volumes, for the fresh European news, and even for the report on miscellaneous literature. We regret that many writers whom we respect and love have refused to participate in Mr. Smirdin's journal and we hope that *The Contemporary* will make up for this shortcoming for us; but we desire that the two journals not try to hurt each other and that each act in its own way for the general good and for the pleasure of a zealous reading public." (209)

This appeal for cooperation between the two journals is double-edged. A. B. does not thank Senkovskij for the articles and fiction of Baron Brambeus (his *nom de plume*), presumably the work which Senkovskij himself most esteemed, but for editorial matters like variety, news, and thickness of volume. And the fact that established writers, including Puškin,[20] refused to contribute to *The Library* is of course discrediting.

Other journals besides *The Library* were dealt with in Gogol''s essay. A. B. continues by offering comments on Gogol''s essentially critical views of three periodicals: *The Northern Bee (Severnaja pčela), Supplements to the Invalid (Pribavlenija k "Russkomu invalidu"),* and *The Telescope.*

Turning first to *The Northern Bee* Puškin, through A. B., is able to present his own criticism of the journal's editor, Faddej Bulgarin (whose reputation today lies primarily in his polemical battles with Feofilakt Kosičkin), criticism of which Kosičkin would have been proud. Bulgarin's attacks on Puškin's work had continued sporadically, though not so sharply, up to this time, regardless of his defeat at the hands of Kosičkin four years earlier. Again the "offended provincial" theme stands out:

> "It is not for advertisements that *The Northern Bee* should be rebuked, but for the inclusion of boring essays with the signature F. B. which (in spite of your disdain for the taste of poor provincials) we have long since evaluated according to their merit. Be assured that it is extremely vexing for us when we see that Messrs. the journalists suppose they can interest us with moralistic issues filled with the most childish thoughts and banal little jokes — which *The Northern Bee* probably inherited from *The Industrious Bee.*" (210)

Although the allusion to advertisements constitutes an indirect attack (*The Northern Bee* could not legally sell advertising space — but sold it anyway),[21] the evaluation of Bulgarin's literary and critical work is explicit.

A. B. refers to *Supplements to the Invalid* only to point out an apparent contradiction in Gogol''s argument, his praise for exactly that manner of writing (humorous critiques) which he condemned in Senkovskij. A. B.'s remarks about *The Telescope,* quoted earlier, relate only to Gogol''s failure to mention the young Belinskij.

Summarizing A. B.'s discussion of Gogol''s essay, we can conclude that he objected to its inconsistencies; but far from giving the kind of defense of Senkovskij one might expect from a provincial, A. B. actually strengthened Gogol''s arguments where he could, particularly in the matter of the pronouns *sej* and *onyj.* After all, A. B. had initially described Gogol''s article only as being slightly inconsistent and "bitter" toward Senkovskij. Of the five issues A. B. selected as Gogol''s accusations against Senkovskij, only the third and fourth were seriously considered in the letter and of these two, one turned out to be a consideration not of Gogol''s errors but of Senkovskij's whole theory of language.

The fifth point was a rather curious one: neither Gogol' nor Belinskij was blaming *The Library* for having too many readers; their difficulty came in explaining the phenomenon. After seeking such an explanation, they naturally came to the same conclusion: the reading public that supported *The Library* could not be very perceptive and discriminating. And it was in this way that Gogol' and Belinskij unwittingly prepared for A. B.'s entrance. With the berating of the provincial landowner by these two journalists, A. B. was conceived.

Puškin chose to use a persona to dispel widespread misconceptions about his journal. The kind of a character this persona had was determined to a great extent by the essays of Gogol' and Belinskij. Obviously someone from the provinces would be an ideal defender of the taste and judgment of provincials and, as a persona, he could serve polemical purposes relating to Puškin's taste as well. These purposes included openly criticizing the infamous Bulgarin, and laying before the public reasonable views about language.[22]

In character A. B. showed himself to be an indefatigable reader, very much concerned about recent developments in journalism. He has his own opinions and when called upon to support them he demonstrates his point in a logically convincing manner. He writes well, is able to stylize, to be serious, to be amusing, and to be cutting. He conceives of literary criticism as a serious activity with a tone determined by the nature and quality of the work being considered. He reads sermons as well as journalism, though he is bored with the petty moralizing of Bulgarin. He also shows himself as being aware of current editions of poetry as well as new poets when he responds to Gogol''s claim that the public had recently shown signs of indifference to poetry: "But isn't poetry always the pleasure of a small number of the elect, while stories and novels are read by everyone everywhere? " (210) As a counter-argument he refers to the great number of editions of Deržavin and Krylov that have come out, and also the recent excitement over Kukol'nik, Benediktov, and Kol'cov.

In his tactics A. B., following in the footsteps of Kosičkin, turns the arguments of his opponents against them, and is very quick to point out inconsistencies. Finally, on a different level, he is a very subtle writer, leaving traces of irony everywhere, particularly with regard to his being a "humble provincial."

Though A. B. and Belinskij, in contrast to Gogol', could recognize that to achieve such a striking success with the public Senkovskij had to possess some skills as an editor, A. B. and Belinskij could not but disagree on the fundamental reason for *The Library*'s success, *viz.*, its appeal to the low standards of provincials. Puškin is clearly using irony at the expense of Belinskij when he has his persona say in his opening remarks about Gogol''s article: "You in it formulated wittily, sharply, and straightforwardly very many just observations." (206-07) Belinskij had written, in his basically positive review of the first issue of *The Contemporary*, that the author's (Gogol''s) "judgments were formulated not only sharply, wittily, and clearly, but even impartially and nobly," and that "in general this article contains many just observations, expressed intelligently, wittily, nobly, and directly."[23] In that the persona's letter was dated by Puškin "April 23," which suggests that it was written before Belinskij's review appeared, perspicacious readers would see that A. B. arrived at a characterization of Gogol''s article nearly identical to Belinskij's. Such a similarity in judgment could only enhance the reputation of provincials.[24]

Whatever the merits of Gogol''s individual opinions, his essay created a controversy and undoubtedly stimulated subscriptions. There is no evidence that Puškin regretted having placed Gogol''s essay in the first volume; there is reason to believe, however, that he did not find it desirable to have his journal identified with a program centered on countering the influence of *The Library*.

Although Puškin showed himself as quite willing to have his journal carry on polemics (especially against Bulgarin and *The Northern Bee*),[25] he indicated that full and direct warfare with the most popular periodical of the time was not a prudent course for a new journal. In any case, there was no need for him to become personally identified with the ignoble position of "following at the heels of *The Library*," and for that reason he appended his editorial note to A. B.'s letter. The concluding lines of the letter and Puškin's editorial statement are given below:

> "And finally: You reproach our journalists for not saying to us: what was Walter Scott? What is present-day French literature? What is our public? What are our writers?
>   Indeed, extremely interesting questions! We hope that in the future you will resolve them, and that in your criticism you will avoid the shortcomings you so sternly and so justly condemned in the essay which we are right to call the program of your journal.*"

And from the editor:

> "*Including A. B.'s letter here with pleasure, I find it essential to give my readers a few explanations. The essay, 'On the Trend of Journal Literature' was printed in my journal, but it does not follow from this that all the opinions expressed in it with such youthful liveliness and straightforwardness are completely in accord with my own. In any case, it is not and could not be the program of *The Contemporary*." (211)

The strong editorial stance taken here demonstrates that Puškin wished to establish that he was an editor independent of the views expressed in his journal. His editorial comment was designed to indicate that the views of his contributors did not necessarily reflect his own. Thus, his use of a persona served a didactic function (among others): both Gogol' and Belinskij were tactfully informed of the editor's policies in regard to contributors, and A. B.'s "expectations" (that the sphere of activity of *The Contemporary* would be broader and nobler than was suggested in Gogol'''s essay) were implicity affirmed. The key to Puškin's editorial position was that he could not be accused of denying or subscribing to the positions of his contributors. By using a persona, Puškin created a context appropriate for the expression of his editorial position with respect to contributors and *The Contemporary*'s program. The effect on the sensitive Gogol' of his reservations about Gogol'''s essay was cushioned, since criticism of individual points did not come directly from Puškin, and the denial that the essay represented the program of *The Contemporary* was given in a note that showed respect for the views of contributors, yet expressed adherence to the principle that the editor's views were fundamentally independent of those of contributors. Offsetting the effect of the essay on the public — especially its implications that *The Contemporary* would engage in polemical warfare with *The Library* – was obviously of concern to Puškin. Being upbraided by an unknown provincial reader presumably would not be as painful to Gogol' as direct criticism from Puškin himself. But there were other advantages to using a persona.

Puškin knew well the polemical potential of a persona through his experience with Feofilakt Kosičkin. As editor he could seemingly remain above polemical skirmishes by letting his persona score polemical points against *The Library* and *The Northern Bee*, while at the same time explicity denying in a separate editorial statement, that his journal would be belligerently polemical. Through his persona he offered well-reasoned discussions of topical issues, such as the pronouns *sej* and *onyj* and the popularity of *The Library*, without presenting himself as a target for personal attacks, which were all too common in journalistic polemics of the day. He could also appeal to provincial readers for subscriptions by flattering them indirectly: A. B. not only could subtly and effectively express Puškin's views on literary issues and personalities of the day without involving Puškin himself, but also could illustrate the intelligence, wit, and seriousness of provincial readers who had been receiving rather bad treatment from periodicals envious of *The Library*'s popularity in the provinces.

Finally, in a roundabout way and without appearing patronizing he could criticize and educate both Gogol' and Belinskij about the role of an editor vis-à-vis contributors; he could present an objective evaluation of the young critic, pointing out his immaturity as well as his energy, without explicitly choosing sides in the controversy over Belinskij's merits. Puškin could have stated his editorial policies concerning the views of contributors without using a persona. The context provided by A. B.'s letter, however, facilitated his explanation of editorial policy by offering at least one reader's impressions of *The Contemporary*, and thereby demonstrating his own sensitivity to his readers' judgments.

From the above it seems clear that Puškin's efforts to acquire Belinskij's services did not necessarily mean that he had come to the same literary and ideological position as Belinskij. Puškin was interested in increasing his readership, and Belinskij had shown himself to be an exciting and engaging polemicist and critic with an earnest style, enormous energy, and a tirelessness which Puškin could make use of, especially since Gogol' had left for Europe after the appearance of the first issue. It is reasonable to assume that during his trip to Moscow in May of 1836 Puškin was actually seeking someone with more journalistic experience to replace Gogol'. Finding no one who was willing to collaborate among the "Observers," Puškin turned to Belinskij. Naščokin's letter to Puškin (in late October or early November) represents concrete evidence of Puškin's plan to have Belinskij join him, but it also reveals something about the relative unimportance of ideology in journalism of the time:

"Even though it's common knowledge, I have to tell you this and, if possible, help. Belinskij was getting 3 thousand from Nadeždin, whose journal has already been closed down; *The Observer* offered him 5 — Greč also called him. Now if you want, he's at your service — I haven't seen him — but his friends, including Ščepkin, say that he will be very happy if he has a chance to work for you. Give me the word and I'll send him to you."[26]

What is interesting here, aside from the fact that Puškin apparently never "gave the word," is that *The Moscow Observer* also wished to employ Belinskij, despite his having been its sharpest antagonist.

It is not difficult to determine why journals would be interested in acquiring a controversial polemicist like Belinskij. *The Contemporary* had about 800 subscribers in 1836 (compared with *The Observer*'s 400-600, *The Telescope*'s 400-600, and *The Library*'s 5000). Judging by the number of copies of each issue of his journal that Puškin had printed (2400 of volumes 1 and 2, 1200 of volume 3, and 900 of volume 4), one can conclude that Puškin had been extremely hopeful of success at the outset.[27] His early letters also reflect this hope. Figures available on his expenses, however, indicate that he was losing money. Although it is certainly true that Puškin had to make some changes in order to increase his journal's circulation, there is too little evidence to warrant claims that the changes involved his ideological and esthetic views in any significant way. Belinskij's virtues as a critic who could draw a large audience — people who were presumably reading *The Telescope* but not *The Contemporary* — could outweigh any ideological differences he might have with the editor, as long as it was clear (and Puškin made it clear in his editorial note to his persona's letter) that no contributor necessarily spoke for the editor or determined the program of the journal.

There is little doubt that Puškin valued Belinskij as a critic. It was reported by Annenkov (who heard it from Belinskij) that Puškin had once said: "Belinskij had lessons even his revilers could afford to learn."[28] On the other hand, differences in ideology and sensibility between Puškin and Belinskij were not negligible. Puškin's persona A. B. referred to the critic's talent, independence of mind, wit, and promise, but also to his need for more knowledge, prudence, and maturity.[29] Even though Belinskij was the only critic to say anything good about Puškin in the 1830's, it was he who announced that Puškin's star was fading and that Gogol' had replaced Puškin as the "leader of Russian poets." Belinskij in reviews and articles had been highly critical of Puškin's predecessors, and had praised recently printed books (such as Polevoj's historical works) which we know Puškin did not highly value. In addition to this, Belinskij's well known affinities for German idealism in this period of his development were not shared by Puškin. Moreover, Belinskij had announced, in his review of the second issue of *The Contemporary,* that his worst fears had been realized and that Puškin's journal had succumbed to the same upper-class arrogance and condescension (*svetskost'* and *aristokratizm*) exhibited by *The Observer.* Puškin could not run a journal successfully, in Belinskij's opinion, because he did not have the all-embracing genius of a Goethe.[30]

Evidence usually offered to support the case that Puškin was drawing nearer to Belinskij in esthetic and social views seems, on analysis, to be rather weak. For example, much has been made of Puškin's so-called "defense" of Belinskij in his article entitled "M. E. Lobanov's Opinion About the Spirit of Literature, Foreign and Our Own," which was printed in the third issue of *The Contemporary* (without Puškin's name). The minor writer and dramatist Lobanov had recently made a speech to the Russian Academy in which he criticized contemporary literature and literary criticism, and called for stronger censorship. Quoting extensively from the printed version of the speech, Puškin challenged most of Lobanov's arguments in his article. He was less critical, however, of Lobanov's assessment of literary criticism. Lobanov said:

> "Criticism, the modern instructress and conscientious friend of literature, had turned into street-corner buffoonery nowadays, into literary piracy, into a way of making a living from the pocket of weak-mindedness by means of audacious and violent sallies — often even against men of the government, celebrated both for civil and literary services. Nothing is respected — neither rank, nor intelligence, nor talent, nor age."[31]

Lobanov's indignant speech on the immorality of literature and criticism could be explained, at least in part, as his reaction to Belinskij's very unfavorable review of his tragedy, *Boris Godunov* (1835). Belinskij was particularly immoderate and patronizing in his criticism of this work: not only did he regard the play as dated, artificial, and unnatural, but he considered the author pitiable: "He works honorably, conscientiously, but he is laughed at; he understands no one, and no one understands him. I cannot imagine a more horrible position."[32] Furthermore, Belinskij's well-known negative views of eighteenth-century writers could have served as a target for Lobanov's charges that literary critics had no respect for the past.

If Lobanov's remarks about the immorality and even criminality of recent literature and criticism, and his call for more censorship, could be so construed as to apply to Belinskij, then Puškin's article could be read as a defense of the critic. The fact remains, however, that Puškin seemed to agree that recent literary criticism tended to be immoderate and to have little respect for tradition. In his article on Lobanov's speech Puškin noted that Russian literature, which is still relatively young, "rarely maintains the solemnity and decorum peculiar to it; perhaps its decisions are often inspired by calculation and not by conviction. Disrespect for names sanctified by fame (the first sign of ignorance and weak thinking) is unfortunately not only considered permissible among us, but even praiseworthy boldness." (189-90) Unless it can be demonstrated that Puškin, speaking anonymously and cautiously because of the severity of the censor, was not giving his real opinion, his reply to Lobanov's speech can only in an extended sense be seen as a special defense of Belinskij.[33]

Even though Belinskij and Puškin may have agreed on general issues relating to censorship and immorality in recent literature, this agreement did not necessarily extend to their opinions of recent books. Their views markedly diverged, for example, on the merits of Sylvio Pellico's *On the Duties of Man,* a collection of pious reflections that had just been translated into Russian. Belinskij's review, which appeared first, treated the book in a mock serious fashion, punning first and then calling the author a grown child who, with his commonplaces, could be useful to the many grown-up children in Russia.[34] In an article later in 1836 Belinskij briefly discussed Ševyrev's positive review of the same book (in *The Moscow Observer*), and reaffirmed his own position that Pellico's commonplaces were childish. Ševyrev's argument, that Pellico had the right to offer truisms and moral lessons because he had suffered a great deal in prison, was countered by Belinskij's comment that commonplaces are commonplaces, no matter who writes them.

Puškin's review of the book, like Ševyrev's, was extremely positive:[35] he even quoted several lines from the latter's review in *The Moscow Observer*. Referring to Ševyrev's arguments about the book's value, Puškin remarked that Pellico did not need the excuses offered by *The Moscow Observer,* for his book could easily stand alone. Thus despite Puškin's reservations about Ševyrev's "excuses," his position on the general merits of the book was basically the same as Ševyrev's and diametrically opposed to that taken by Belinskij. Moreover, without identifying him by name, Puškin described Ševyrev as a "writer of true talent, a critic who deserves the confidence of enlightened readers." Whether we should take all of Puškin's words here at face value may be open to question, but there can be little doubt that on the surface they do not support Belinskij's views of Pellico's book. Evidence that Puškin wished to set himself apart from other members of his class and align himself with "democratic" factions represented by Belinskij can hardly be found in his very mild criticism of Ševyrev here.

The point of introducing examples of apparent differences between Puškin and Belinskij is to illustrate that the sharing of similar views was not, to Puškin, a precondition for successful collaboration. To be sure, they were substantially in agreement on more important issues such as the merits of Gogol' and the shortcomings of Benediktov. Nonetheless Puškin's efforts to bring Belinskij to *The Contemporary* could not be said to constitute his personal acceptance of Belinskij's esthetics, which were then strongly idealist. This is not to say that Belinskij's views would not have had an effect on Puškin had they begun to collaborate.[36] One can speculate on whether Puškin's patience would have survived the critic's trek from Schelling to Hegel and then to Saint Simon. If Puškin had made an offer to Belinskij, it would have implied above all his desire to have working for him a talented and energetic young writer who could attract more readers to the journal. That an offer would imply no more than this was the message sent by way of Puškin's persona and his editor's note. In addition to avoiding polemical warfare with *The Library for Reading* and showing good will toward provincial readers, Puškin and his persona tactfully set out a basic rule for participation in his journal: contributors do not necessarily speak for the editor. Taking advantage of the situation created by misinterpretations of the significance of Gogol''s essay, Puškin turned what could have been understood as a mistake in editorial judgment into an illustration of a modern editorial policy. These goals could not have been achieved easily without the help of a secret persona-author.

The preceding analysis of Puškin's persona has sought to provide some understanding of the complexity of the journalistic situation and an appreciation for the difficulty of drawing conclusions about ideological matters. Puškin used A. B. as a means of educating Belinskij and other contributors; this education was part of Puškin's tactical plan to enlist Belinskij's support as a contributor but at the same time to make clear his independence as editor. Even allowing for Puškin's recognition of the growing importance of *raznočincy* in Russian letters, and his sensitivity to changing social currents, there is hardly sufficient reason to conclude that he was prepared to let Belinskij carry the ideological banner of *The Contemporary*.

The analysis was also designed to provide a better understanding of Puškin's creativity as exemplified in his journalistic creation, the provincial A. B.. The offended provincial played an important role in the expression of *The Contemporary*'s editorial policy, and indirectly Puškin's esthetics, and provided us with suggestive material pertaining to the relationship of two of the most prominent figures in nineteenth-century Russian letters.

NOTES

1. Puškin's use of a persona in *The Telescope* has been studied by J. Thomas Shaw, "The Problem of the Persona in Journalism: Puškin's Feofilakt Kosičkin," in *American Contributions to the Fifth International Congress of Slavists,* Volume II: Literary Contributions (The Hague: Mouton, 1963), 301-26. I am aware of no previous separate study of Puškin's "A. B.," although A. B. is often discussed in Soviet scholarship dealing with *The Contemporary.*

2. Puškin's authorship was first discovered by V. P. Krasnogorskij in 1916, but his arguments were published only posthumously in 1924, "Novaja stat'ja Puškina (Puškin o Gogole)," in *Naš trud,* I-II (Moscow, 1924), 106-19; Krasnogorskij's arguments were substantially reworked by Ju. G. Oksman in "Pis'mo k izdatelju g. A. B." in *Atenej,* I-II (Leningrad, 1924), 15-24.

3. Principal works consulted on the topic of Puškin and Belinskij are: V. G. Berezina, "Iz istorii *Sovremennika* Puškina," in *Puškin: Issledovanija i materialy,* I (Leningrad: AN SSSR, 1956), 278-312; M. P. Eremin, *Puškin – publicist* (Moscow: "Xudož. lit.," 1963), 344-407, and the second edition (Moscow: "Xudož. lit.," 1976), 356-414; F. Ja. Prijma, "Puškin i Belinskij," *Russkaja literatura,* No. 1 (1977), 30-46; I. V. Sergievskij, Puškin i Belinskij," in his *Izbrannye raboty* (Moscow: Goslitizdat, 1961), 215-330; Ju. G. Oksman, "Puškin – literaturnyj kritik i publicist," in A. S. Puškin, *Sobranie sočinenij* (Moscow: Goslitizdat, 1962), VI, 441-69; Nikolaj Smirnov-Sokol'skij, *Rasskazy o prižiznennyx izdanijax Puškina* (Moscow, 1962), 444-46; and N. L. Stepanov, "*Sovremennik,*" in *Očerki po istorii russkoj žurnalistiki i kritiki,* I (Leningrad, 1950), 402-14.

4. For a discussion (and bibliography) of the topic Puškin and Gogol', see N. N. Petrunina, G. M. Fridlender, "Puškin i Gogol' v 1831-1836 godax," in *Puškin: Issledovanija i materialy,* VI (Leningrad: AN SSSR, 1969), 197-228.

5. Prijma (38), Sergievskij (278), and Berezina (293) see A. B.'s remarks as essentially positive, while Eremin, though seemingly agreeing in this assessment, is more cautious, mentioning but not explaining the possibility that Belinskij indeed did not have Puškin's maturity with respect to literary matters (406-07). All further references to Eremin will be to the second edition (1976).

6. The text of Gogol''s "O dviženii žurnal'noj literatury v 1834 i 1835 godu" may be found in vol. VIII, 156-76, of his *Polnoe sobranie sočinenij* (Moscow: AN SSSR, 1938-52). Berezina (284) describes initial reactions to the essay.

7. Puškin prepared the way for A. B.'s letter by announcing in the second issue of *The Contemporary* that he had received an article from Kosičkin and a letter from A. B., and that both would be printed in the third issue. The article from Kosičkin never appeared.

The texts used in this study are from the seventeen-volume edition of Puškin's works, *Polnoe sobranie sočinenij* (Moscow, Leningrad: AN SSSR, 1937-59). Puškin's letter may be found in XII, 94-99. English translations of his critical writings are from *The Critical Prose of Alexander Pushkin,* ed. and trans. by Carl Proffer (Indiana University Press, 1969). Page numbers in the text refer to this edition. Unless otherwise noted, other translations in this study are my own.

8. The reasons why Gogol' did not mention Belinskij in his survey are discussed by Sergievskij (315n), Eremin (384), and Berezina (298). Gogol' may have felt that it was indelicate to speak of a critic who had praised his work.

9. *The Letters of Alexander Pushkin,* trans. J. Thomas Shaw (3 vols.: Indiana University Press and University of Pennsylvania Press, 1963), III, 769.

10. Naščokin's letter may be found in Puškin, *Polnoe.* . ., XVI, 181.

11. Pogodin's remarks concerning Puškin and Belinskij are given in M. Poljakov's short article in *Ogonek,* 60 (1950), 24. Also relevant here are Belinskij's recollections (in a letter to Gogol' in 1842) of favorable comments Puškin made about him to others; V. G. Belinskij, *Polnoe sobranie sočinenij,* XII (Moscow: AN SSSR, 1938-52), 109.

1.2. Sergievskij demonstrates convincingly that Puškin was well aware of Belinskij's writings (224-29).

13. See especially Belinskij's "O kritike i literaturnyx mnenijax *Moskovskogo nabljudatelja*" (1836), II, 123-77.

14. See Puškin's letters of May 4, May 11, and May 14-16 (in *The Letters.* . ., 761-65, 767).

15. See, e.g., Ju. G. Oksman, "Perepiska Belinskogo: Kritiko-bibliografičeskij obzor," in *Literaturnoe nasledstvo,* 56 (Moscow: AN SSSR, 1950), 233-34; Eremin, 408-10; Sergievskij, 313 ff; and Prijma, 45.

16. Referring to the readers of *The Son of the Fatherland,* Gogol' said:

"These readers and subscribers were respectable and elderly people living in the provinces, for whom something to read was as essential as taking a nap for an hour after dinner, or shaving twice a week." (VII, 164)

Belinskij, in "Ničto o ničem," II, 7-50, was even stronger:

"I said that the secret of the constant success of *The Library for Reading* lies in the fact that this journal is essentially *provincial,* and in this regard it is impossible to be surprised at the craftiness, and the intelligence, at the art with which it adapts itself to and ingratiates itself with the provinces." (19)

Belinskij's tone becomes more and more sarcastic as he proceeds in this article to characterize the typical provincial family and the manner in which it dutifully follows the different departments of *The Library for Reading.*

17. Eremin, 397-400.

18. Eremin's statement (402) that Puškin and Belinskij were basically in agreement here is somewhat misleading. Strictly speaking, the editor's relationship with contributors is a "domestic" matter; nevertheless, this does not mean that Puškin himself was not concerned about editors who "corrected" or "improved" works of contributors, and, Eremin aside, it is doubtful that he viewed complaints about this editorial practice as reflecting only the limited perspective of Gogol' and the editors of *The Moscow Observer.*

19. See Prijma's discussion of Belinskij's views on this issue (39-41); these pronouns have since fallen from use in the literary language.

20. Puškin speaks of his refusal in a letter to Naščokin in early 1836:

"My financial circumstances are bad — I have been forced to undertake a journal. I don't know yet how it will go. Smirdin is already offering me fifteen thousand to renounce my undertaking and become again a collaborator of his *Library.* But though that would be profitable, I nevertheless cannot agree to it. Senkovskij is such a knave and Smirdin such a fool that one cannot have anything to do with them." (*The Letters.* . ., 748.)

Puškin had published in *The Library* before (e.g., "Pikovaja dama" in 1834).

21. Eremin, 405.

22. Distinguishing between Puškin's and A. B.'s views may pose some problems, but there is much that is clear. Obviously Puškin is not himself a "humble" provincial, although Puškin shares with his persona a fondness for irony; furthermore A. B.'s views of literature, various periodicals of the day, and writers associated with these periodicals may be identical. Where their views presumably differ is on the issue of Gogol''s article as a program for *The Contemporary.* To say that in the matter of the "five points" A. B. shows his true character

as a somewhat simple-minded provincial (Berezina, 296n) is to misjudge A. B.'s (if not Puškin's) irony and polemical powers.

23. Belinskij, II, 181, 183.

24. Berezina (285) noted the similarity in wording, but no one has noted the possibility that Puškin was being ironic here at Belinskij's expense.

25. Berezina, 287-90.

26. Puškin, *Polnoe. . .*, XVI, 181.

27. Smirnov-Sokol'skij, 446-47.

28. P. V. Annenkov, *The Extraordinary Decade: Literary Memoirs,* ed. Arthur P. Mendel, tr. Irwin R. Titunik (Ann Arbor: University of Michigan Press, 1968), 261. Annenkov also says the following about Puškin and Belinskij:

> "Both Puškin and Gogol' were regarded with extreme favor by the critic but they maintained an obstinate silence about him practically throughout their lives. The former, as reported by Belinskij himself, merely secretly sent him issues of his *Contemporary* and remarked about him: 'That strange fellow for some reason is very fond of me.' " (5)

29. Interpretation of A. B.'s assessment of Belinskij is a complex issue. Berezina (293) views the comments as essentially positive, since they seem more favorable than what Gogol' had planned to say in his essay. Sergievskij (277-78) argues, however, that Puškin and Belinskij were in basic agreement on all the fundamental literary issues of the day, but Puškin as a tactical move had A. B. state conventional reservations about the critic which had been expressed in even stronger terms by Belinskij's enemies. Eremin, with perhaps the most balanced view of the matter, states that A. B.'s remark represented Puškin's true feelings, that the remark was benevolent, that it was offered in a tone not at all like the one in which A. B. expressed his views of Bulgarin and Senkovskij, that it represented criticism of the verbal attacks on Belinskij by Bulgarin, Senkovskij, and Vjazemskij, and that it contained friendly advice (which Belinskij could learn from) relating to the "deep historicism" of Puškin's later literary views (407). Even though Eremin is virtually alone in suggesting that it was Puškin's views that largely prepared the way for the later views of Belinskij, and that Belinskij lacked the "deep historicism" of the mature Puškin, he nonetheless maintains that their ideological affinities (386-90) inevitably (*zakonomerno*) led to their mutual desire to collaborate (414).

30. Sergievskij, in an extensive discussion of the views of Puškin and Belinskij, states that they agreed more often than not on eighteenth- and nineteenth-century Russian writers, that they had basically the same esthetic views (despite Belinskij's philosophically "idealist" phraseology), and that their views were "embryonically" related to the materialist esthetics of Černyševskij (250-51). Puškin, according to Sergievskij, was moving in the direction of Belinskij (321), and inviting him meant that Puškin was asking not only for a contributor but an ideologue of *The Contemporary* (216). In a similar vein, Berezina (293-96) discusses the ideological affinities of the two; also see Oksman, "Puškin. . .," 460, and "Perepiska. . .," 233.

The obvious problem is the difference in philosophical provenience of the two which of course determined their essentially different esthetic views. For a discussion of the esthetics of Puškin and of Belinskij (in his Schelling period) which suggests that they have little in common, see Victor Terras, *Belinskij and Russian Literary Criticism: The Heritage of Organic Aesthetics* (Madison: University of Wisconsin Press, 1974), 24-25, 54-59.

31. Puškin cited this passage in his article on Lobanov; see *The Critical Prose. . .*, 189.

32. Belinskij, I, 210-11.

33. Cf. Sergievskij, 279-84; Oksman, "Puškin. . .," 46-61; and Eremin, 397. Eremin suggests that Puškin was actually arguing with Gogol' and Odoevskij, not Belinskij.

34. Belinskij, II, 88-89.

35. *The Critical Prose. . .,* 203-05. Previous scholarship (e.g., Berezina, 296) has tended to emphasize Puškin's distance from his aristocratic acquaintances, in this case Ševyrev. In view of the fact that Puškin valued good criticism charitably expressed, it is possible that he regarded the personal nature of Belinskij's critical style as an indication of the critic's lack of "maturity."

36. There is no evidence, however, that their relationship would have involved significant mutual compromise, as Sergievskij (305) and Prijma (46) state.

TOLSTOJ AND KANT

Gary R. Jahn, University of Minnesota

This account of Tolstoj's acquaintance with and use of Kant is not an "influence study." With the probable exception of Rousseau, who was the fascination of Tolstoj's youth, it would be difficult to show that Tolstoj's opinions were influenced by any writer, if "influence" implies change or notable growth. This is not for want of documentary evidence attesting to Tolstoj's thorough awareness of Russian and foreign literature, but rather because of the great pride which he took in the independence of his thoughts and his untiring determination to find his own way through the besetting confusions of his life and art.

Tolstoj was much more likely simply to use (perhaps to abuse) the thoughts of other writers than to be influenced by them. Zenkovsky wrote that "Tolstoj began to philosophize very early, but he did not receive a systematic education in philosophy. . . There was much that was *accidental* in his philosophic enthusiasms during various periods — accidental in the sense that he was influenced by books that happened to fall into his hands. But all of his enthusiasms corresponded to his own, distinct or indistinct, searchings."[1]

Thus, a level of interest which might suggest influence in the case of another writer is, in Tolstoj's case, generally no more than the recognition of a kindred spirit. The present paper provides an account of Tolstoj's developing acquaintance with Kant's ideas and demonstrates the rather considerable extent to which those ideas, as Tolstoj understood them, overlapped with his own. I also suggest that Tolstoj's eventual overt enthusiasm for Kant is no more than the final stage of his lifelong sympathy with the wisdom which he acknowledged only in his declining years to be, in fact, Kantian.

In an early draft of his *Confession* (*Ispoved'*, 1882) Tolstoj wrote: "Philosophy had always interested me. I loved to follow the intense and graceful movement of thought by which all of the world's complex phenomena were joined together, in all their diversity, into a single whole."[2] His interest, however, was or soon became less than passionate. As a student at Kazan' University in the 1840's he participated very little in such intellectual circles as then existed there and preferred the less spiritual joys of youth: he did his lessons (often badly) and had a good time (XXXIV, 397).

His philosophizing was later described in *Boyhood* (*Otročestvo*, 1854) as "work beyond my strength" (*trud neposil'nyj*). His efforts led only to a vicious circle of constant analysis accompanied by weakness of the will and a diminution of the freshness of feeling (II, 57-58). He summarized the process in the pithy phrase "Um za razum zaxodil," which may be rendered as "Mind would get the better of reason." The distinction between "mind," the powers of logic and unaided thought, and "reason," cognition based upon a broader foundation where the heart and the head cooperate, did much to encourage his enthusiasm for Kant when he discovered it later on in the *Critique of Practical Reason*.

Tolstoj soon turned completely away from speculative philosophy and toward what he called the "science of life." He believed that life ought to be a process of inner-directed self-formation rather than the pursuit of external goods.[3] He wrote: "But if all people would be concerned with perfecting themselves, then the social order could in no wise be disturbed, for everyone would be doing for others that which they desired others to do for them" (I, 229). Such an idea provided a firm foundation for Tolstoj's later sympathy with Kant's categorical imperative, although it is, in its present formulation, an obvious allusion to the Golden Rule of the Gospels.

It has been shown that Tolstoj was familiar with Fichte's *Science of Knowledge* (1794-95),[4] but his acquaintance with other German philosophers seems to have been sketchy. He considered Schelling morbidly subjective,[5] and he consigned Hegel to the graveyard of the useless and incomprehensible. In *What Then Should We Do?* (*Tak čto-že nam delat'*, 1886) he wrote: "When I was young Hegelianism was the basis of everything. It was borne in the very air... Everything rested upon it, but now forty years have passed and not a bit of it remains. No one gives it a thought and it is as though it had never been" (XXV, 332). Still stronger is the remark that he had tried to read Hegel but that he was unable to understand him (*dlja nego èto byla kitajskaja gramota*).[6] Tolstoj made no documented reference to Kant prior to 1862.

It is unlikely that before 1869 Tolstoj possessed any exact knowledge of Kant's thought. Probably he knew little more than that Kant was a German philosopher who flourished at the end of the 18th century and was known for his ponderous style and the opacity of his thought. In an article of 1862, for instance, he classes Kant with the despised Hegel ("O narodnom obrazovanii," VIII, 8), and in an early published variant of the first volume of *War and Peace* Andrej's reading of Kant was used to suggest one of the facets of his overweening pride (IX, 449).

In August, 1869, however, Tolstoj wrote to Fet that a revolution had been wrought in his thinking by reading Schopenhauer and mentioned that through Schopenhauer he had also begun to understand and appreciate Kant (LXI, 219). "Kant" at this time means the ideas expressed in the *Critique of Pure Reason*. Tolstoj's "ecstasy" with respect to Schopenhauer and his enthusiasm for Kant were, however, soon replaced by a more temperate attitude which was engendered and nourished by his perception of their ideas as essentially negative and pessimistic. Consequently he soon began to seek some relief from their conclusions. At one point in the early 1870s he considered art a possibility in this respect.[7]

Tolstoj remained reserved toward Kant through his "crisis" and discovery of the wisdom of Jesus. To Tolstoj in the 1870s Kant's greatest contribution was his introduction of the concepts of space, time, and causality as categories of the mind. He accepted, if with reluctance, this view of reality and regarded Kant as a partial ally in the battle against materialism. In a draft of *Confession* he reproached both Kant and Schopenhauer for failing to give specific answers to ethical questions such as "What should I do? " and "Why should I do it? " (XXIII, 499). His attitude emerges most clearly in a fragment, "A Debate in the Kremlin on Faith" ("Prenija o vere v Kremle"), which he wrote in late 1877 and early 1878 and later expanded under the title "The Interlocutors" ("Sobesed-niki"). The participants represent various points of view: one is a clergyman, another a materialist, and so on. Tolstoj designated the first of his participants as "Strem[ov]: idealist philosopher; Kant, Schopenhauer, Straxov, Fet" (XVII, 369). Stremov acts as the opponent of the materialist and thus, for Tolstoj, plays a positive role. But Tolstoj also wrote himself into the discussion, under the name "Ivan Il'ič," in order to express his dissatisfaction with some of the features of "Idealism."

His ambivalence toward Kant continued through the mid-1880s, but in 1887, after reading the *Critique of Practical Reason,* his attitude became vastly more positive. Tolstoj's sympathy with this work was comparable in intensity to his regard, as a youth, for Rousseau, his initial discovery of Schopenhauer, and even to his reverence for the Gospels. On 13 October he wrote to N. Ja. Grot that he had just read the *Critique of Practical Reason* for the first time and was in a state of "joyous rapture" (*radostnoe vosxiščenie*) (LXIV, 104). On the previous day he had expressed similar thoughts in a letter to P. I. Birjukov, adding that he intended to translate or paraphrase certain portions of the work. His most extensive remarks are in a letter of 16 October to N. N. Straxov. After setting forth his emotional reaction to the book, he indulged in a brief tirade against that "scribbler" (*pačkun*), Schopenhauer, who had led him to believe that the *Critique of Pure Reason* was the summit of Kantian thought. In fact, he continued, that work was no more than a polemic with Hume and served to clear the ground on which Kant raised the "temple" of wisdom which was the *Critique of Practical Reason* (LXIV, 105-06).

Tolstoj was unable to understand how the world could have accepted the *Critique of Pure Reason* and rejected the *Critique of Practical Reason.* He saw at once that his former attitude to Kant, developed through the mediation of Schopenhauer, was incorrect. He abandoned the view that Kant was a negativist concerned only with abstract speculation and began to regard him as a great "religious teacher," *i.e.* as a teacher of morality.

Tolstoj's admiration for Kant reached its zenith in 1896. In his notebook for July of that year he entered the brief note "Christ and Kant" (LIII, 284). Thus he suggested that the essence of Kant's philosophy was identical with the teaching of Christ. He developed the comparison further in an entry in his diary for 30 July: "Kant, we are told, caused a sharp turn in human thought. He was the first to show that things as they really are in themselves are inaccessible to knowledge, that the source of knowledge and of life is spiritual. Well, isn't that the very same thing that Christ said two thousand years ago, but in a way which people could understand? " (LIII, 103).

Tolstoj came eventually to believe that the best philosophy of all ages formed an essential unity, and, from 1896 until the end of his life, Kant held a pre-eminent place in his mind as one of the great thinkers of history and perhaps the greatest philosopher of the modern period. More and more (there are dozens of references) Kant's name became an indispensable part of a litany of the great teachers — Socrates, Buddha, Christ, Spinoza, Amiel, Emerson — whom Tolstoj viewed as his conscious allies against the twin evils of materialism and formalism. There are even a few references from this period which suggest that Tolstoj saw himself consciously, if perhaps facetiously, as a figure similar to Kant. He often expressed his admiration for Kant's simple style of life and claimed that he was experiencing feelings which he believed Kant to have shared (LXXXVIII, 247-49). He was no doubt also aware that they both enjoyed the reputation of great teachers of their time and were commonly perceived as geographically localized: the Sage of Königsberg and the Sage of Jasnaja Poljana.

In 1905 Tolstoj became familiar with one more of Kant's works: *Religion within the Limits of Reason Alone.* By now, however, no further intensification of agreement with Kant was possible. We find such comments as "Kant is very close to me" and "I am intensely in awe of him" (LV, 162; LVII, 79; LV, 13). This book only confirmed Tolstoj's attitude toward Kant.

Tolstoj's last reference to Kant dates from February, 1910. "How I value Kant," he said, "but he is so heavy."[8] Thus, Tolstoj's final estimate of Kant was that he knew the truth, was in essential agreement with that long line of great teachers of whom the greatest was Christ, had added to the sum of human wisdom especially by his concepts of the freedom of the will and the conditional nature of the reality of space and especially of time, but who, unfortunately, expressed himself obscurely and could be understood only with difficulty.[9]

The most convenient indices of the ideas which Tolstoj most valued in the work of Kant (or any other writer, for that matter) are the miscellanies which he edited in the period after his conversion and especially in the last decade of his life. In these volumes Tolstoj collected the thoughts and exhortations to virtue of famous persons, both past and present.

The miscellanies exist in various lengths and formats. Some are brief collections of the sayings of individual thinkers and derive such unity as they have from the single source from which they proceed. Others are longer and organized in the manner of the lives of the saints, with a certain amount of material, drawn from various sources, appointed to be read on a given day of the year. In a few cases the organization into daily readings is supplemented by grouping the extracts by general subject or by adding longer weekly or monthly readings.

Tolstoj's first miscellany was "A Calendar of Proverbs for 1887" ("Kalendar' s poslovicami na 1887 g."), which he prepared in 1886. This work was compiled from folk wisdom on the basis of the printed collections of Snegirev and Dal' as well as Tolstoj's own notes and observations. It offers a selection of proverbs for each day of the year and contains no editorial commentary. In 1895 Tolstoj lent his hand to a second compilation, a volume of the collected sayings of John Ruskin.

The efflorescence of Tolstoj's interest in miscellanies, however, came only in the last decade of his life, during which the compilation of such works was a steadily increasing source of activity. In 1903 he published *The Thoughts of Wise People for Every Day* (*Mysli mudryx ljudej na každyj den'*) and in 1907 several volumes containing extracts from individual thinkers, persons as diverse as La Bruyère, Vauvenargue, La Rochefoucauld, Mohammed, Krishna, and Lao-Tse. Finally, in 1908 and 1910 respectively, he completed his most ambitious endeavours in this line: *The Cycle of Reading* (*Krug čtenija*) and *For Every Day* (*Na každyj den'*). These compilations required five years of intermittent labor into which the entire Tolstoj household, even more than usual, was drawn. Also in 1910 Tolstoj published his final book of this type. Entitled *The Way of Life* (*Put' žizni*), it is similar to the two preceding in format but much reduced in size.

Tolstoj selected and presented the thoughts of the great thinkers with an unashamed and even doctrinaire subjectivity of method. In the preface to one of the larger miscellanies he ridiculed the scholarly precision which seeks to preserve every nuance of the original in its translations, even to the point of rendering that which is coarse, clumsy, or unclear in the original in like manner in the translation. Considering such niceties appropriate only to pedants, Tolstoj freely rephrased, abbreviated, and occasionally even interpolated explanatory matter into the texts which he presented. The extracts are generally identified only by author and were in most cases taken not from original sources but from similar earlier collections, mainly volumes of English manufacture. The only clue which Tolstoj provided to the extent of his interference in the wording of a given passage was his practice of identifying reasonably direct translations (which, most often, were translations of translations) only by the author's name. Passages which he had rendered more freely were identified with the formula "According to X," for example, "According to Kant" (*po Kantu*).

Tolstoj's approach to the compilation of the miscellanies corroborates Èjxenbaum's assertion that he cared nothing for the system developed by a given thinker, but only for the support of individual ideas.[10] He used an occasional saying even from such a thinker as Nietzsche, whose ideas as a whole he completely rejected.

Tolstoj first employed Kant's ideas in a miscellany of 1903 which was wholly devoted to the sayings of Kant and Lichtenberg. The later and larger miscellanies contain very numerous Kantian citations, in many cases the same quotations, or variants thereof, being shared by all three, i.e. *The Cycle of Reading, For Every Day,* and *The Way of Life.* Tolstoj's main source for these quotations was a collection of Kant's sayings, published in Leipzig in 1901 under the title *Ausspruche: Zusammengestellt von Dr. Paul Richter.*

The presence of Kant's ideas in the miscellanies is, relatively speaking, very extensive. The indices to volumes 40-45 of the Jubilee Edition of Tolstoj's works (wherein are printed the chief miscellanies) contain more than 140 references to Kant. His presence is exceeded only by Ruskin, Pascal, and Marcus Aurelius and far surpasses Rousseau and Schopenhauer.

Tolstoj often reused the same quotations in the various miscellanies, occasionally with minor changes in wording. For example, Kant's epitaph "The starry sky above me, the moral law within me" is repeated no less than five times in the various miscellanies.[11] Thus, the large number of references to Kant represents a smaller number of particular quotations and a still smaller number of general concepts which these quotations were selected by Tolstoj to illustrate.

Tolstoj used Kantian sayings in connection with six basic themes: 1) religion, 2) knowledge, 3) the character of the age, 4) the nature of man, 5) death and suffering, and 6) art. Given Tolstoj's low opinion of Kant's literary style, it is not surprising that paraphrase predominates over translation in the presentation of his ideas in the miscellanies.

With respect to religion Tolstoj approved Kant's idea that there is one true "rational religion," consisting solely of moral precepts, in which all particular religious creeds participate to a greater or lesser extent. Kant's categorical imperative was Tolstoj's favorite statement of the essence of the moral law.[12] He cited it repeatedly in the miscellanies, preferring the simple paraphrase: "Act in such a way that you can say to everyone: act as I have" ("Postupaj tak, čtoby ty mog skazat' každomu: postupaj tak, kak ja" XLI, 333). Tolstoj also used Kant to affirm that a person's relation to God is knowable only in the sphere of action and that the only way to please God is by leading a morally good life.

In addressing the theme of knowledge Tolstoj drew upon Kant to explain the difference between mental and rational knowledge (*umstvennoe i razumnoe poznanie*). The words "mental" and "rational" are the usual English equivalents but may in the present case seem either misleading or senseless. *Um,* which I shall call "mind," meant for Tolstoj the organ which performs abstract philosophical thinking. His disbelief in the sufficiency of mind, which he identified with Kant's "pure reason," was obvious as early as the 1850s (see above). Tolstoj preferred to rely rather on *razum,* which might best be translated by the 18th-century concept of "right reason."[13] It was Tolstoj's lifelong distrust of the purely mental which led him as a young man to ignore Kant, whom he knew by reputation as concerned with the operation of pure reason. Thus, it is easy to explain his sudden immense enthusiasm for Kant following his discovery of the *Critique of Practical Reason,* for he found there an appeal to right reason defined as an inborn moral sense which, when combined with the operations of mind, yielded a practical guide to right conduct.

Besides explaining and approving the practical or right reason, the miscellanies devote some attention to exposing the inadequacy of pure reason or mind. Especially important for Tolstoj were Kant's notions of the vastness of space which, since it is one of the categories of the mind, can never be exhausted and the conditional (or conventional) nature of time (*uslovnost' vremeni*).[14] Tolstoj used these ideas to suggest the illusoriness of all perceivable phenomena and the consequent importance of that moral knowledge which alone was able to bring man into contact with the absolutely real.

Tolstoj shared Kant's apparent dissatisfaction with the times and customs and often drew upon him to criticize the spirit of the age. It is an age preoccupied with mere phenomena and lacking genuine moral wisdom. It is dominated by a meagerness of spirit which has led to such consequences as the improper teaching and rearing of the young[15] and the inequitable distribution of wealth along with the misguided concept of philanthropy proceeding from it. The only virtue of the age was its proclivity for criticism, and this, if applied in the pursuit of wisdom rather than mere knowledge, might yet lead to salvation. In this way Tolstoj implied that Kant was the greatest of modern philosophers since criticism (*i.e.* the critical philosophy) was so closely associated with his name.

Tolstoj quoted from Kant in depicting man as a being whose great capabilities suggest a higher destiny than that of the animals. It is proper to dissociate man's spiritual essence from the coarse requirements of animal existence. The chief of man's higher capabilities is transcendental freedom, which is understood as the only "thing in itself" which can be directly perceived, but only through the practical reason. Tolstoj developed the idea of transcendental freedom asserting itself in the face of empirical determinedness as early as *War and Peace,* and he understood Kant to be a firm supporter of it. Human beings are also described in the miscellanies as having an innate need for work and Kant's saying that the purest joy is that found in rest after labor is repeated frequently. Man is essentially a creature of duty and the only genuinely good pleasure is that obtained in the unexpected and spontaneous interstices of the performance of moral obligations.

The problem of death was of major concern to Tolstoj and, especially in his later works,[16] he commented on the difficulty of realizing the inevitability of death. He quoted Kant with approval to the effect that human beings are unmoved by the thought of death because they are by nature active. Consequently death, the absolute cessation of activity, is a difficult and perhaps incomprehensible subject of meditation.[17] Suffering, on the contrary, has a positive value as a powerful force in the motivation of self-discovery. This idea is present in such works as "God Sees the Truth, But Waits" ("Bog pravdu vidit, da ne skoro skažet," 1872) and *The Death of Ivan Il'ič* (*Smert' Ivana Il'iča,* 1886) wherein the protagonists are driven by suffering to an awareness of what they have been and what they ought to be.

For Tolstoj there was a fatal flaw in Kant's aesthetic theory: the naming of beauty as the salient characteristic of art. In a draft of *What is Art?* (*Čto takoe iskusstvo,* 1898) he wrote: "According to Kant, for example, who has given us a more exact definition, art is the human activity which produces *Wohlgefallen,* which pleases without the help of concepts [*ponjatija*] and does not evoke desire. And this definition would have been fully exact and comprehensible, if only that which produces *Wohlgefallen* had not been defined as beauty" (XXX, 316). He found support in Kant for the ideas that true art possesses a moral content and that it is precisely the universal moral content which permits the artist and the audience to become one in the shared experience of the work.

Tolstoj's substantial agreement with Kant, as he understood him, extends over a considerably broader range of topics than previous commentators have allowed. Masaryk, who provided the most detailed account of Tolstoj's relationship to Kant, detected only two significant points of resemblance between them: 1) their insistence upon morality as the essence of religion and 2) their perception of the individual as transcendentally free.[18] The present analysis augments this list. Tolstoj was clearly in sympathy with the broad outlines of Kant's deontological ethics. He shared with Kant the distinction between practical reason (right reason, *razum*) and pure reason (mind, *um*), and this distinction is crucial not only for his later religious teaching but also motivates Levin's musing (in *Anna Karenina*) that even though he "knows" that it is the earth and not the stars which moves, yet he is right to affirm that he is the still point around which the stars are turning. Tolstoj also found much of value in the concept of space, time, and causality as categories of the mind. This is especially true of the concept of time, for which Tolstoj acknowledged his debt to Kant. Finally, despite his disagreement with the use of beauty as the basic aesthetic criterion, he found ideas of value also in Kant's theory of art.

The opinion of Tolstoj as one who eschewed influence but welcomed support is certainly valid. He rarely did have and perhaps could not have ideas that were not, in some sense, his own. We must recognize that his relationship with Kant is essentially not different from his relationship to any other thinker or writer. All were of interest to him only insofar as they confirmed or sharpened his own thoughts.

It is clear that the ideas of Kant which Tolstoj came to value so highly were nearly all thoughts which he had previously worked out for himself, mainly in his youth and certainly by the time of *War and Peace.* Observing them in the miscellanies is a valuable review of ideas which already existed at the early stages of Tolstoj's career, perhaps malformed or still in embryo but present nonetheless. A knowledge of Tolstoj's later views may, then, be very helpful in attaining a full and proper appreciation of works from any period in his career, and it is likely that our understanding especially of *Anna Karenina* and *War and Peace,* which antedate Tolstoj's enthusiasm for Kant by ten and twenty years respectively, will benefit greatly if they are considered from the point of view of the ideas which Tolstoj shared with Kant. Tolstoj's affinities to Kant range over a whole gamut of ideas: epistemology, metaphysics, ethics, and aesthetics as well as the criticism of the age. For this reason, Kantian ideas as seen through Tolstoj's eyes may well provide a key to the fuller understanding of Tolstoj's work as a whole.

NOTES

1. V. V. Zenkovsky, *History of Russian Philosophy*, trans. G. L. Kline (London: Routledge, Kegan Paul, 1953), II, 390-91.
2. L. N. Tolstoj, *Polnoe sobranie sočinenij* (Moscow: GIXL, 1928-58), XXIII, 499. Further references to Tolstoj's writings are noted in the text and are all to this edition. In the present connection see also the memoir of N. Bulič as contained in a letter to N. Grot published in *Varšavskie universitetskie izvestija*, 9(1912), 67-68. A further, although less reliable, source for Tolstoj's youthful attitude to philosophy is the *Trilogy*, especially *Youth* (e.g. II, 343-44).
3. B. M. Èjxenbaum, *Lev Tolstoj: Semidesjatye gody* (Leningrad: Xud. lit., 1974), 215.
4. Èjxenbaum, *70-ye gody*, 214.
5. See chapter 19 of *Boyhood* in which the hero describes the time wasted in his efforts, under the influence of Schelling, to turn around suddenly enough to catch nothingness *"le néant* — there where I was not."
6. B. N. Čičerin, *Vospominanija: Moskva sorokovyx godov* (Moscow: M. and S. Sabašnikov, 1929), 217.
7. From Tolstoj's notebook (12 March 1870): "The history of modern philosophy. Descartes strongly, surely overturns everything and builds again, dreamily and willfully. Spinoza does the same, Kant the same, Schopenhauer the same. But why build? The work of thought leads to the hopelessness of thought. There is another weapon — art. Thought demands numbers, lines, symmetry, movement in space and time, and by these destroys itself... Art and art alone knows neither the categories of time and space nor motion — only art, always inimical to symmetry and the circle, gives the essence." (XLVIII, 18.)
8. N. N. Gusev, *Letopis' žizni i tvorčestva L. N. Tolstogo: 1891-1910* (Moscow: GIXL, 1960), 745.
9. In "Why Do Men Stupefy Themselves?" ("Dlja čego ljudi odurmanivajutsja?," 1890) Tolstoj wrote: "But why is it that people who drink and smoke often manifest the highest qualities, both mental and spiritual? The answer to this is that... we do not know what heights these drinkers and smokers might have achieved had they not been drinkers and smokers... It is very probable, as an acquaintance of mine was saying, that Kant's books would not have been written in such a strange and poor style, if he had not smoked so heavily." (XXVII, 227.)
10. "Tolstoj took no interest at all either in the system of Belinskij's views or in their evolution; as in other cases also, he read Belinskij in order to find support for his own thoughts." (B. M. Èjxenbaum, "Nasledie Belinskogo i Lev Tolstoj: 1857-58" in his *O proze: Sbornik statej* (Leningrad: Izd-vo Xud. lit. [Leningradskoe otdelenie], 1969), 136.)
11. E. Kuprejanova, in her *Èstetika L. N. Tolstogo* (Moscow-Leningrad: Izd-vo Nauka, 1966), had demonstrated that Tolstoj's interest in this quotation was already apparent in *Anna Karenina* (see pp. 106-110).
12. See Tolstoj's letter of 1 May 1904 to A. F. Koni (LXXV, 96).
13. Here is Tolstoj's version of the distinction between *um* and *razum*: "Mind and reason are two completely different qualities. Mind is the ability to understand and comprehend as conventions the conditions in which we live (*sposobnost' ponimat' i soobražat' žiznennye, mirskie uslovija*); reason, on the contrary, is the divine spark which reveals to the soul its relationship to the world and to God. Reason is not only not the same thing as mind, but is even its opposite; reason frees man from the temptations (deceptions) to which mind subjects him. The main activity of reason is that in defeating these

temptations it liberates love, the essence of man's soul, and makes it possible for love to manifest itself." (XLIII, 163.)

14. In Tolstoj's diary (22 September 1904) we read: "Kant's basic idea of the will as a thing in itself, outside of time, is perfectly correct and known to all religions (the Brahmin), but expressed more simply and clearly. One thing more remains, but that a tremendous service: the conditional nature of time (*uslovnost' vremeni*). That is really great. One feels how far behind one would be if one had not, thanks to Kant, understood this." (LV, 13.)

15. Tolstoj now finds himself in sympathy with Kant as an educator, in contrast to his negative view of the early 1860s.

16. But also throughout his career. See my "L. N. Tolstoj's Vision of the Power of Death and 'How Much Land Does a Man Need? ,'" *SEEJ*, XXII, 4(Winter, 1978), 442-53.

17. In the early story "Three Deaths" ("Tri smerti," 1858) the most blessed of the three protagonists is the tree, which is not conscious that it is dying.

18. Thomas G. Masaryk, *The Spirit of Russia: Studies in History, Literature, and Philosophy,* trans. E. and C. Paul, 3rd impression (London: George Allen and Unwin, 1961), III, 171, 191.

PART II

STUDIES OF INDIVIDUAL WORKS

THE QUEEN OF SPADES: A PARODY OF THE HOFFMANN TALE

Roberta Reeder, Harvard University

Introduction

If ambiguity and possibilities of a multiplicity of decodings by different generations of scholars mark the richness of a work, then Puškin's *The Queen of Spades* fulfills this criterion. The approaches are sociological, psychological, philosophical, and formalist.[1] While various relevant insights reflected in these interpretations will be taken into account, the focus of this article will be a formalistic one. It will examine *The Queen of Spades* as a parody of literary tradition, in particular, of the Hoffmann tale. A structural typology of the Hoffmann tale will be presented which is based on the schemata evolved by V. Ja. Propp but which identifies componential units and patterns specific to the Hoffmann tale which are often different from that of the fairy tale, on which Propp based his analysis.[2] Puškin's tale will then be investigated to see whether it imitates these components or directly negates them with transmogrified versions.

Certain critics find specific motifs and characters in European stories similar to those of *The Queen of Spades*. Yet they do not discuss these stories as reflecting a coherent literary system with predictable elements. Nor do they see any parody of such a system in Puškin's tale.[3] Others mention elements of parody of specific works. Galina Bžova relates Lizaveta to Karamzin's Liza, and she becomes the false deceived bride. Germann is presumably derived from the character of that name in Goethe's *Hermann and Dorothea*, and becomes a false romantic lover, a false demonic fighter for an idea. The work as a whole, then, becomes a set of false semiotic signs.[4] Andrej Kodjak points to another possible literary reference for the story, Goethe's *Faust*. The countess represents Mephistopheles and Germann becomes Faust, but unlike his prototype, he is deprived of free will and cannot alter the course of his actions through repentance. In Kodjak's view, the story is a theological vision of the world, a play with the Faustian sign system, a godless model of the universe.[5] V. Vinogradov suggests the tale is a parody of French "frantic novels," and notes Germann is often more ridiculous than brave.[6]

Some interpretations see a relationship between *The Queen of Spades* and the Hoffmann diabolical tale, but often reveal a misunderstanding of what the Hoffmann tale is really like. James Bayley says that in Hoffmann and Balzac there is a straightforward fantasy of the supernatural which gives power to the possessor but finally destroys him.[7] On the contrary, many Hoffmann stories are marked by an ambiguity as to the actual existence of the supernatural. Bayley notes the comic nature of Germann, a victim as much as villain, and refers to the exchange of letters in the story as a parody of *Clarissa*.[8] Both N. L. Stepanov and B. N. Botnikova assume that the supernatural is basic to the Hoffmann tale, whereas in Puškin's work the events are finally given a realistic explanation. Botnikova goes so far as to say Puškin totally rejects Hoffmann's artistic discoveries.[9] Charles Passage sees the possible influence of Hoffmann's "The Sandman" (a hero predisposed to madness) and "Gambler's Luck" (about a compulsive gambler), but says the actual influence of either work on Puškin is minimal. He says the story is not a parody, but a profound depiction of the struggle between mind and idea; an idea possesses the hero and triumphs over his sanity.[10] Norman Ingham also says *The Queen of Spades* is not a parody of Hoffmann, nor is it an acceptance of Hoffmann's romantic world-view, although there are evident borrowings from his stories which include gambling.[11]

Some critics point out the debunking of the characters without mentioning any relation to the Hoffmann tale. V. Xodasevič views Germann as a "Petty Prometheus," appropriating the laws of real heroes but without achieving their level; the hero uses supernatural knowledge only as a means of getting rich. While he may have the "profile of Napoleon," he is far from having the "soul of Mephistopheles."[12] In his analysis of the epilogue in respect to the rest of the tale, J. T. Shaw points out that Germann is both demonic and vulgar, Lizaveta is both a martyr and looking for a savior so she may become like her patronness, and Tomsky is content with hardly golden mediocrity.[13] J. D. Clayton sees the story as a parody of Faust and a travesty of the Oedipal relationship, but mentions no parody of Hoffmann.[14]

Thus the range of criticism about the relationship of *The Queen of Spades* to the Hoffmann tale is from one of total lack of influence to a superficial borrowing of motifs without the philosophical basis of the genre. Others see certain elements of the tale as parody, but not in relation to the Hoffmann tale. To establish the possibility of such connections, one must examine first how pervasive Hoffmann was in Russian literature of the period, then testimony to Puškin's expressed opinion of the tales; then the actual components of typical Hoffmann tales will be examined to determine if and how they are employed in Puškin's work.

Hoffmann in Russia in the 1820s and 1830s

Izmajlov notes that by the mid-1820s the fantastic genre was popular in Russia.[15] Hoffmann was first translated in 1822, when his "Mademoiselle de Scudéry" was published. Antonij Pogorelskij's "The Poppyseed-Cake Woman of the Lafërtov-Quarter" (1825) was the first Russian story imitating Hoffmann. The years 1830-1833 witnessed the peak in Hoffmann's popularity in Russian periodicals. Stories based on his tales by Vladimir Odoevskij and Nikolaj Polevoj appeared, translations of his tales were published, and numerous articles appeared.

Puškin's library contained several translations of the Hoffmann tales.[16] William Lenz describes Puškin's enthusiasm for Hoffmann at a soirée in 1833:

"Puškin talked of nothing but Hoffmann; it is not in vain that he wrote *The Queen of Spades* in imitation of Hoffmann, but with more refined taste."[17] Critics generally link three stories by Puškin to Hoffmann. One is "The Lonely Cottage on Vasilevskij Island" where many of the motifs and characters resemble Hoffmann's *Datura fastuosa*.[18] Puškin's "The Undertaker" which is a story in *The Tales of Belkin* (1831) is also mentioned as having a possible relation to the Hoffmann tale, but this relation has not yet been demonstrated.[19] Yet many of the stories in *The Tales* are literary parodies, and there are so many features common to both "The Undertaker" and the typical Hoffmann tale that it would be difficult not to see it as a conscious parody of the latter. *The Queen of Spades* has much in common with those Hoffmann tales in which the existence of the irrational is ambiguous. A discussion follows of the various tale types in Hoffmann's corpus, and then *The Queen of Spades* will be examined for its similarities and contrasts to these tales.

The Hoffmann Tale

The Hoffmann tales are *Kunstmärchen* or "art fairy tales." They are not versions of tales collected from the folk, but original works with supernatural elements, and which convey philosophical insights into man and nature.

Typical features basic to the Hoffman tale are:

The Irrational

The irrational plays different roles in the tales. Todorov's distinction between the uncanny, the fantastic, and the marvelous will help in interpreting these different roles. In the uncanny, irrational events are given realistic motivation at the end of the story; the marvelous posits the existence of the irrational as a basic component of the universe; the fantastic, however, hovers between the two:

> The fantastic . . . lasts only as long as a certain hesitation: a hesitation common to reader and character, who must decide whether or not what they perceive derives from "reality" as it exists in the common opinion.[20]

The role of the irrational divides the Hoffmann tale into two basic types. In one the supernatural world is accepted as a premise, and thus reflects Todorov's "marvelous." In others the role of the irrational is ambiguous, and realistic motivation is provided for possible irrational events. In both tales, however, three possible worlds are usually portrayed: the everyday world, the spiritual world, which is further divided into the demonic, and the world of truth and beauty. The Philistine is either entirely closed off to the spiritual world or attains a brief encounter with the demonic aspect of it, then only to consciously suppress it. The artist is in touch with both aspects of the spiritual world. In the tales the spiritual world is not removed from reality, but pervades it, and

Wolfgang Kayser sees this very aspect of the tales as producing the grotesque effect so typical of them.[21]

Duality

One typical structural pattern in the Hoffmann tale is duality. One such duality is the choice of the artist between the everyday, secure world of the Philistine and the spiritual world which may lead him to the demonic and destructive or to the artistically creative. This is the basic duality within the *Doppelgänger*, the literary type which since Hoffmann has become so important in European literature. Other relevant oppositions upon which the tales are structured are God/Devil, instinct/intellect, Germany/Italy. As Arthur Gloor notes, there is no way out of this duality, but in some characters consciousness has given them the freedom to observe it and come to terms with it.[22]

Dreams — Through dreams supernatural forces are revealed or hidden psychological desires are made manifest.

Synesthesia — the simultaneous excitation of different sensations and their association was part of the romantic conception of the essential unity of all sense perceptions, and on a higher level, of the basic harmony of all of nature.

Madness — this is often the result of the attempt by the hero to make contact with supernatural forces. It is as if it is a price to be paid for learning nature's secrets. In one of the conversations which appears in *The Serapion Brothers*, Cyprian says, "I always believed that in the abnormal, nature vouchsafes to us glimpses into her most terrible depths."[23]

The Occult — this includes mesmerism, somnambulism, and clairvoyance. Whether Hoffmann actually believed in the occult is difficult to determine. What is important is that it entered into his aesthetic repertoire in his literary works.[24]

Italy — "Italiensehnsucht" or a "longing for Italy" became symbolic for a longing for a land where freedom and the arts flourished, in contrast to Germany, the land of the Philistine.

Automata — in some tales automata appear, representing mechanical, illusory manifestations of the spirit.

Satire — satirical attacks against contemporary German society in general and sometimes specific people in particular are typical of Hoffmann's works.

It is important not only to isolate the various components and aspects of the Hoffmann tale, but to examine how they are employed within a system. As several critics have pointed out, many motifs are double-edged and may lead either to spiritual creativity or destruction. The occult can be used for achieving good, but also for attaining power over a victim; art can lead to spiritual calm or to asphyxiation; fantasy may inspire the imagination or lead to total escape from the real world; the energy of the unconscious can be creative when kept pure and restrained, but is destructive when it rages out of control.[25]

Hoffmann was brilliant in his description of realistic detail, which, however, does not prevent his tales from remaining essentially typical of Romanticism.

This should be kept in mind when reading criticism which points to *The Queen of Spades* as an example of Realism because of Puškin's mastery at describing contemporary Russian life with such accuracy. Hewett-Thayer discusses this aspect of Hoffmann:

> He was an observer in two worlds and in the Märchen he fused two worlds with sovereign skill. With Hoffmann the reader walks up and down the streets of Dresden, Berlin, and Frankfurt, enters perhaps in his company into familiar restaurants and cafes; and these experiences are as realistically and vividly portrayed as in the realistic novel of a later day. But in the Dresden cafe the Archivarious Lindhorst, who is really a salamander, talks of his ancestors, the lily and the youth of Phosphorus; the coat tails of the old gentleman may perhaps become wings and bear him away.[26]

The structuring of time and space is complex in the Hoffmann tale. Often the story begins in the present, in contemporary Germany. Either the immediate or distant past is introduced at relevant points in the story. There is frequently a brief epilogue telling the reader the eventual fates of the major characters. Episodes from the past may occur in Italy, and mythological passages occur in mythological time and space. Often there is a frame story, with a brief episode in the present which sets up a situation which motivates the telling of the tale about an event in the past which is somehow related to the present.

What is not mentioned by critics discussing Hoffman's influence in Russia is that Hoffman himself wrote several works of self-parody, and Puškin certainly could have read them in his French translations. "The King's Bride" is a delightful satire on the Romantic poet, the Eternal Feminine, and the ivory-tower mystic, and the entire story is a parody of Hoffmann's tales in which erotic relations exist between mortals and supernatural beings, as in "The Golden Pot." "The Sandman" is a more tragic version of parody, where the hero, as Germann in *The Queen of Spades*, is a petty Prometheus in touch with the spiritual, but incapable of achieving great heights, and ends up going mad.

Schemata

The following is a componential analysis of the major character types and functions which appear in Hoffmann's tales. Propp defines function in the following way: "Function is understood as an act of a character, defined from the point of view of its significance for the course of the action."[27] Each function will be designated by a letter of the alphabet. As in Propp, although the initial situation is not a function, it will be designated by a letter since it is an important morphological element of the tale. In addition, the letters "b," "c," and "d" will stand for situations where the positive spiritual dominates, the demonic dominates, or the Philistine world dominates, and will be placed in a separate column so this particular pattern of contrasts so basic to the tales can be isolated. A third column will list the characters who participate in the function, so one can immediately identify the relationship between given characters, a given function, and the world that dominates. As will be seen below, unlike the fairy tales, the sequence of functions is not always identical, and this marks one of the major ways in which Hoffmann varies the tales. While a large corpus of tales served as the basis for developing the schemata presented here, only a few representative examples will be analyzed for comparison with *The Queen of Spades*. Based on this larger corpus, however, it became clear that a finite set of functions and characters was constant throughout the tales, although not all of them appear in every work. The time pattern will also be analyzed, and segments of time such as "present" and "immediate past" will be assigned temporal designations. Propp's schemata also allows for description of features that distinguish one character type from a similar character type by physical and spiritual qualities, nomenclature, and sex. These features will be discussed at the beginning of the presentation of the analysis of each tale, where the character types are always introduced.

This analysis does not pretend to exhaust an interpretation of either the Hoffmann tale or Puškin's work. Propp also pointed out that his morphological analysis only focused on certain aspects of the fairy tale, that it was a useful model for the kinds of information he was trying to elicit, but that other models were valuable for looking at other aspects of the tale. What is being sought here are abstract components that will aid us in identifying how Puškin's version of the Hoffmann tale is different from and similar to the original genre. By isolating the components from the numerous details in each work, the charts allow us to focus on the constant elements within each of the tales. We will then see if these same components appear in Puškin's story and in what manner they are treated. The components chosen were based on the reading of numerous Hoffmann tales, as mentioned above, and thus were selected by the process of deduction rather than imposed on the basis of an inductive hypothesis.

CHARACTER
TYPES   m – male; f – female

Hero – H
H   Usually *Doppelgänger*, divided between the Philistine and the spiritual.

Villain – V
Vm_1 older male, in direct contact with demonic powers, sorcerer
Vm_2 younger male, usually servant of older villain
Vf_1 older female, often witch, in contact with demonic powers
Vf_2 younger female, usually beautiful, demonic, femme fatale

Philistine — P

Pm_1 older male, usually bourgeois, well-established, interested in power and money, no sensitivity for the arts or spiritual matters.

Pm_2 younger male, at the beginning of his career, but already planning all his actions on the basis of gaining power and wealth. No sensitivity for the arts or spiritual matters

Pf_1 older female, bourgeois, enjoys life of housewife, security more important than the arts and spiritual matters

Pf_2 younger female, usually unmarried, wholesome, wishes secure life with husband who can provide for her, little sensitivity for the arts. May show some initial interest in the irrational, only to finally reject it for security and a peaceful life.

Agent to the Good and the Beautiful — A

Am_1 older male, often seer, good magician using irrational powers for good purposes. Initiates the hero into the good and the beautiful by setting tasks.

Am_2 usually male friend of hero who warns him against the Philistine world and the demonic and urges him to embrace the good and the beautiful.

Af_1 older female who is mother figure, helps hero to attain the good and the beautiful

Af_2 younger female, shows the hero the way to the good and the beautiful, but he must choose to follow her and undergo trials to win both her and this world.

Listener — L

L   Main function is to be audience for the frame story told by the first-person narrator. Sympathetic to what is being narrated.

Mythological Characters — M

Mm   fairy tale hero. Not *Doppelgänger*. He is brave, good, and decisive.

Mf   fairy tale heroine. She is pure, innocent, often the victim of a villain and saved by the mythological hero.

Mv   Mythological villain — usually a fairy tale monster like a dragon.

( ) — when any character is put in parenthesis, it means he is a *deceptive* type. Thus the hero may identify a woman who is really a Philistine as the female agent of the world of the good and the beautiful. While this character could be assigned Pf_2, it is more important for the analysis of the story that she be categorized as (Af_2) so the deception is clear. Thus in "The King's Bride" the parody is based on the pseudo-poet's inability to see that his muse is really quite stupid and totally incapable of understanding anything aesthetic or spiritual. She in turn cannot see his ineptness as a poet.

When there is more than one representative of a particular type, where it is relevant he, she, or they are assigned lower case letters, for example, Pm_{2a} is Heerbrand, a major figure in *The Golden Pot*, and Pm_{2b} are the Philistine young men who choose to remain in their Philistine crystal jars.

FUNCTIONS

Following are the major functions which appear repeatedly in the Hoffmann tales. They do not follow any necessary sequence, and they need not all be present.

a	initial situation (time, place, introduction of characters)
b	positive spiritual dominates
c	demonic spiritual dominates
d	philistine world dominates
d_1	courtship of Pf (philistine woman)
d_2	marriage to Pf
e	deception
$-e$	revelation of deception
f	tempts hero or heroine to commit sin
f_1	commits sin — gambles, murders
$-f$	overcomes temptation to sin
g	receives gift to reach positive spiritual realm
$-g$	receives gift to attain demonic realm
h_0	hero destroyed
h_1	suicide of hero
h_2	hero goes mad
h_3	hero's spirit broken
i	interdiction
$-i$	breaks interdiction
j	awarded by the demonic
k	experiences synesthesia
l_1	courts Af_2 (agent of the good and the beautiful)
l_2	marries Af_2
m	mythological actions
n	realistic motivation provided for seemingly irrational event
o	occult message
o_1	correct interpretation of message
o_2	incorrect interpretation of message
p	task carried out
$-p$	task not fulfilled
q	Philistine inadvertently shows way to spiritual realm
r	has dream

s   combat between the good and the demonic
↑   transference from once place to another
( ) – deceptive function. For example, (o) would be a pseudo-occult message.

TIME SCHEME
P   present
IP   immediate past
DP   distant past
F   future
M   mythical time
Fr   time of frame story

HOFFMAN TALES
The Marvelous
I. The first category is the Marvelous, where it is accepted that irrational forces exist. The hero cannot control the forces, and therefore is ruled by destiny rather than being able to control it by his moral choices.

GAMBLER'S LUCK
Characters: H   Chevalier, poor nobleman. Has always avoided gambling.
            L   Siegfried, young baron, rich. Refused to gamble until now.
            Vm_{2a} Friends of the Chevalier who encourage him to gamble
            Vm_{2b} Dubernet, boyhood friend of Angela
            (Vm_1) Signor Vertua, Angela's father, gambler, said to be usurer
            Af_2 Angela, Signor Vertua's daughter

Chars	World	Functions	
Frame Story			
L	c	a	Summer of 18 .. Pyrmont, spa. Various people taunt Siegfried to gamble.
L	c	f_1	Siegfried gives in and becomes obsessed with gambling, cannot stop.
L,H	b	i	Stranger (H) appears. Tells his story to serve as a warning not to pursue the demonic world of gambling.
Central Story			
H		a	Paris, Chevalier could not afford to gamble, avoids it.
H,Vm_{2a}	c	f,j	Friends persuade him to gamble. He does and wins.
H	b	−f	Chevalier refuses to gamble for a year.

Chars	World	Functions	
H, Vm_{2a}	c	f,j	Chevalier needs money, friends encourage him to gamble. He does and wins. Now continues to play.
H	c	h_3	Gambling destroys Chevalier mentally and physically.
$H,(Vm_1)$	b	i	Vertua comes to table where Chevalier is banker. He is seen by Chevalier's friend as villain. Instead Vertua tries to warn Chevalier against demonic world of gambling.

Vertua's Story

(Vm_1)	c	f_1	Vertua was inveterate gambler. Young man loses fortune at his table, wounds Vertua in attempted murder.
$(Vm_1), Af_2$	b	$-f, \uparrow$	Vertua vows never to gamble again. Goes to Italy. Wife gives birth to Angela, dies. Vertua says he has been falsely accused of usury by profligates who owe him money. He has come to try to save Chevalier.

Central Story

$H,(Vm_1), Af_2$	b	$-f$	Chevalier meets Angela, falls in love. She rejects him. He vows never to gamble again in order to win Angela's love.
H, Af_2	b	l_1, e	Chevalier courts Angela. She thinks she loves him, deceived.
H, Af_2	b	l_2	Chevalier marries Angela.
Af_2, Vm_{2b}	b	$-e$	Angela sees Dubernet, realizes it is he whom she really loves.
$(Vm_1), Af_2$	c	$-e$	Vertua dies. Has not overcome his passion for gambling since it obsesses him instead of listening to the priest. Angela now thinks Chevalier also may go back to gambling.
H, Af_2, Vm_{2a}	c	f	Chevalier begins to doubt Angela's fidelity, "his evil star began to rule." Friend tempts him back to gambling.
H	c	$h_3, \uparrow$	Young man loses at Chevalier's table, commits suicide. Everyone turns against Chevalier. He leaves for Genoa.
H, Vm_{2b}	c	f_1	Chevalier gambles at Stranger's table, continuously loses.

Chars	World	Functions	
H,Af_2	b	i	Angela warns Chevalier not to gamble. He goes for last time.
H,Vm_{2b}	c	$-i,f_1$	Chevalier loses all. Bets his wife, loses her as well.
H,Vm_{2b}	b	$-e$	Stranger reveals he is Dubernet. "The dark spirit revealed to me that in gambling I could ruin you." He had followed Chevalier to Genoa to destroy him. Find Angela dead; H brokenhearted and remorseful.

Frame Story

H,L	c	$-e$	Stranger leaves. Few days later dies of apoplexy. Siegfried learns he is actually the Chevalier.
L	(b)	$-f$	Siegfried vows never to gamble again.

Time Scheme

Fr   P   DP   P   F

In this story the Philistine world does not play a role. All characters are in touch with one aspect of the spiritual world, either the demonic or the good. The story is basically structured around interdictions and breaking of the interdictions. The demonic forces act here through agents such as the hero's friends, and the influence of Af_2 is not strong enough to overcome these forces. Once the hero violates the interdiction, he is in the power of the demonic forces. There is a constant alternation within the story of the two worlds. The hero takes part in most of the episodes, interacting with agents of one of the two spiritual worlds. The tale is masterfully constructed, with the pattern of overcoming/being overcome by temptation paralleled in all three stories. Although Siegfried has not yet been destroyed by the demonic, the implication is that his overcoming of this temptation is deceptive, and he, too, will be the victim of the fate of the others. The levels of time form an interesting pattern, and as many of his tales, Hoffmann introduces a short epilogue after the basic narration telling what happened to the characters.

The Fantastic

II. The second category is the Fantastic, where there is an ambiguity concerning the existence of the irrational. The Philistines in the story provide a rational explanation for events that appear to be irrational.

THE GOLDEN POT

Characters: H	Anselmus, handsome but socially awkward, student and poet
Pm_{1a}	Conrector Paulman, established bourgeois

Pm_{1b} Burgher, who cannot believe in the irrational
Pm_{2a} Registrator Heerbrand, young bourgeois who is trying to become an important administrator and achieve a life of bourgeois security
Pm_{2b} Kreuzkirche Scholar and Law Clerk — young bourgeois who consciously reject the world of the good and the beautiful.
Pf_1 Burgher's Wife, who cannot believe in the irrational.
Pf_2 Veronica, Paulman's daughter, whose goal in life is to marry a good provider and to be a good hausfrau.
Am_1 Archivarius Lindhorst, in touch with the irrational powers and uses these forces for good purposes. He is also the Salamander from the mythological world.
Am_2 Narrator, who has same choices given to Anselmus to accept or reject the world of the good and the beautiful.
Af_2 Serpentina, snake-daughter of Archivarius, who opens the way for Anselmus to experience the world of the good and the beautiful.
Vf_1 Appleseller / fortune-teller / witch. Shrivelled crone with peaked nose, cat-eyes, creaking voice. Uses irrational powers to create havoc in real world.
Vf_2 Mesdemoiselles Oster, friends of Veronica, who urge her to turn to the witch, and thus the demonic.
Mm_1 Phosphorus, Prince of Spirits, like fairy tale hero
Mm_2 Salamander, hero of mythological world who must pay for not restraining his powers, which then become destructive.
Mm_3 Gardener in mythological world
Mf_1 Lily, fairy tale heroine whom fairy tale hero saves.
Mf_2 Snake, with whom Salamander is in love.
Mv Dragon, mythological villain.

Chars	World	Functions	
First Vigil			
H	b	a	Ascension day, 3:00, Dresden
H,Vf_1	c	o	Anselmus runs into applecart, apple seller shrieks, "You'll end up in the crystal!"
H,Af_2	b	o,k	Elder-tree, snakes with confusing speech, synesthesia.
H	d	n	H says this is really the sun sporting in the elder-bush.
Second Vigil			
H,Pm_{1b},Pf_1	d	n	Burgher and wife say H's babbling about vision was caused by liquor.

Chars	World	Functions	
H,Pm_{1a}, Pm_{2a}	d,b	n	Anselmus is invited by Paulman and Heerbrand to the former's house. On the way, Anselmus again sees snakes, then sees this was only fireworks reflected in the water. Paulman says this is the behavior of a madman.
H,Pf_2	d	d_1	Anselmus forgets vision because of attraction to Veronica.
H,Pm_{2a}	d	(q)	Heerbrand arranges for Anselmus to work for Archivarius.
H,Vf_1	c	s,o	At Archivarius' house, Anselmus threatened by doorknocker. Bell-rope becomes serpent, coils around him. Knocker screams prophesy, "To the crystal."
Third Vigil			Story told by Archivarius
$Mm_1,Mf_1,$ Am_1	b	p	Lily falls in love with Phosphorus. To win his love she must leave parents, playmates, endure torture. She will perish at moment of highest rapture and will then give birth to thought. She accepts, and thought is born.
Mv	c	f_1	Dragon appears, captures thought.
$Mv,Mm_1,$ Mf_1	b	s	Phosphorus overcomes Dragon. Lily becomes Queen. She is Archivarius' ancestor.
Pm_{1a},Pm_{2a}	d	n	Paulman and Heerbrand say story is nonsense.
H,Am_1,Pm_{2a}	b	q	Heerbrand brings Anselmus and Archivarius together. Anselmus will go to Archivarius and copy for him.
Fourth Vigil			
H,Am_1,Af_2	b	g	Anselmus insensible to everyday life, goes to elder-bush every day. Once Archivarius appears, shows Anselmus a ring; in the rays he sees Serpentina; he tells Anselmus that if he *decides* to work for him, he will see daughter. He gives him liquid to pour on doorknocker so he may enter the house without danger of demonic forces.

Chars	World	Functions	
Fifth Vigil			
Pf_2	c	o	Shape appears to Veronica behind common household objects. It shrieks, "He will not be your husband!"
Pf_2	d	n	She realizes objects are merely household items, yet still has sense of horror.
Pf_2, Vf_2	c	o,f	Friends urge Veronica to visit Frau Rauerin, a fortune-teller, so she may find out her fate with Anselmus. She goes, but Rauerin tells her Anselmus will never be mayor and does not love her.
Pf_2, Vf_1	d	n, o_2	Veronica interprets the prophesy as babble.
Pf_2, Vf_1	c	o	Rauerin tells her to return on equinox if she is serious about Anselmus as Hofrat and husband.
Sixth Vigil			
H, Vf_1	c, b	s	Anselmus overcomes doorknocker by pouring liquid over her.
H	b	k	Anselmus is surrounded by synesthesia of spiritual realm.
H, Am_1, Af_2	b	p	Anselmus must copy texts in exotic languages. Archivarius warns him that hostile forces will assail him, but from "effort and contest" he can overcome them.
Seventh Vigil			
Pf_2, Vf_1	c	f_1	Veronica visits the witch on the fall equinox, hoping her demonic powers will win her Anselmus. But as Anselmus arises from the cauldron, the witch shrieks, "Bite him to death!" Veronica loses consciousness.
Eighth Vigil			
H, Am_1, Af_2	b	p	Anselmus continues with assigned task. Serpentina appears to him, "By your belief . . . you shall obtain me."
Serpentina — Tale about Salamander			
H, Af_2	b	o,i	Tale told by Serpentina acts as prophesy and injunction.

Chars	World	Functions	
$Mm_1, Mm_2,$ Mf_2	b	i	Salamander falls in love with Snake, the Lily's daughter. Phosphorus warns him that the Salamander's embrace will consume the Snake and a new being will arise.
Mm_2, Mf_2	b	−i	Salamander does not heed the injunction, and prophesy is fulfilled. In desperation, Salamander burns the garden with his flames.
$Mm_1, Mm_2,$ Mm_3	b	o	Gardener asks Phosphorus not to punish the Salamander, since it was love that drove him to despair. Phosphorus extinguishes the Salamander's fire, but says the Salamander will endure man's needs and oppressions while the speech of nature is no longer intelligible to degenerate man. But if three youths understand the song of the three snakes, his daughters, then the Salamander shall rise again into the sacred harmony of Nature.
Mm_1, Mm_3	b	g	Phosphorus gives the Salamander's daughters a present of a golden pot from which his kingdom is mirrored back.
Mv, Vf_1	c	f_1	Dragon is in fetters, but one of his quills mates with a beet and they produce Rauerin, the witch.

Ninth Vigil

Chars	World	Functions	
H, Pm_1, Pm_2	d	n	Anselmus goes to Paulman's. Battle in his soul between the two realms. They all get drunk, and Anselmus misses his day of work at Archivarius'. Drunken philistines are a caricature of what the irrational can release.
H, Am_1	d	n,−p	Anselmus thinks of Veronica. Passes by Archivarius' garden, and finds it ordinary. He makes a mess of his copying task. Archivarius punishes him, and he ends up in crystal bottle.

Tenth Vigil

Chars	World	Functions	
H, Pm_{2b}	d		Anselmus realizes difference between him and the two others in the bottles. They choose to be in this symbol of the Philistine

Chars	World	Functions	

world. Because they do not know what freedom and love are, they do not feel the
oppression of their imprisonment by the Salamander.

H, Af_2, Vf_1, Am_1	b, c	s	Direct confrontation between good and evil forces. Serpentina urges Anselmus to believe; the witch says he will never escape. Anselmus says he will give up becoming Hofrath in his love for Serpentina. The Salamander overcomes the witch in a struggle between them.

Eleventh Vigil

Pm_1, Pm_2	d	n	Heerbrand blames Anselmus for bringing out the irrational at their party. Calls Anselmus mad. For several months both Heerbrand and Anselmus disappear.
Pm_2, Pf_2	d	n, d_2	Heerbrand reappears, has been made Hofrath. Veronica becomes his wife, rejects Satanic arts. Heerbrand says Veronica's story of Anselmus and Serpentina is poetic allegory.

Twelfth Vigil

Am_1, Am_2, Af_2, H	c	l_2	Narrator receives letter from Archivarius, learns Anselmus is now a true poet, lives with Serpentina. Narrator visits Archivarius in his realm, Atlantis; Anselmus tells him Serpentina has brought him the lily, which is the knowledge of the sacred harmony of all beings. Narrator returns to garret but knows the poetical possession of his inward sense is part of Atlantis.

Time Scheme

P   M   P   M   P   F

The Golden Pot is one of Hoffmann's greatest tales. Here the full panoply of functions and characters is explored. Structurally there is a constant alternation between the Philistine world and the spiritual world of the demonic and the good. The hero is present in most scenes, being tempted by the various agents of these three worlds and having finally to make the decision of whether to have security and a normal life, or live blessed by poetry and the gift of insight into the harmony of nature, and be considered mad and alien by most people. In the sections concerning the mythological world, the Salamander plays a role similar to that of Anselmus. He must also bear certain burdens and earn his way back into the kingdom of Atlantis. The other sections where Anselmus does not appear are devoted to Veronica, who represents the Philistine attempting to encounter the irrational, but turning to the negative rather than positive aspect of it, and finally rejecting it for the sake of both material and psychological security and comfort. The time scheme alternates between present and mythological time, and the story ends with a brief projection into the future telling us of the fate of the characters.

Parody

III. The third category is parody. Here the characters are ridiculous or incompetent versions of what they pretend to be — poets, seers, women of spiritual beauty or demonic purpose. The functions become cheap imitations of actions normally engaged in by seers, poets, etc.

THE KING'S BRIDE

Characters: (H) Amandus. Someone at the university told him he was a poetic genius. His verse actually wallows in sentimentality.

(Am_1) Herr Dapsul von Zabelthau. Tall, gaunt; performs astrological operations in his tower.

(Af_2) Anna, his daughter. Her specialty is vegetable gardens. In love with Amandus.

(Vm_1) King Daucus Carota, Carrot King in love with Anna.

(Pf_2) Anna's maid, who does not believe in the irrational.

Chars	World	Functions	
Chapter I			
$(Am_1)(Af_2)$	(b)	a	Bountiful year in small village where Zabelthau and Anna live.
$(H)(Af_2)$	(b)	(1_1)	Amandus sends Anna a letter with atrocious poem. At end he adds, "O lofty virgin, do not forget to send me Virginian tobacco." Anna does not understand the poem, and assumes "roots of love" means "a red carrot."

Chars	World	Functions	
Chapter II			
(Am_1)	(b)	(o)	Zabelthau does astrological mapping of Amandus/Anna relationship. Sign of great danger, but Amandus will save his bride.
$(Af_2)(H)$	(b)	(g)	Anna writes Amandus letter (which acts as gift from female agent of spiritual to the hero). She includes one of her own poems, which is worse than his.
(Af_2)	(c)	(o)	Pulls carrot, finds mysterious ring around it.
(Pf_2)	d	n	Maid says ring was in ground and carrot grew through it.
$(Am_1)(Af_2)$	(b)	(o)(s)(i)	Zabelthau performs ritual to find out about ring. He wears false beard, and resembles Father Christmas. Discovers wealthy gnome in love with Anna, but Anna is unworthy since she pickles sauerkraut instead of deciphering horoscopes.
Chapter III			
$(Vm_1)(Am_1)$	(c)	e	Carota arrives, builds palace. Zabelthau finds him charming. Anna will not marry him.
$(Af_2)(H)$	(b)	s	Anna writes Amandus for help; wants him to challenge Carota to a duel.
Chapter IV			
$(Vm_1)(Af_2)$	(c)	e	Carota begs for Anna's love. In his tent she sees enormous vegetable garden, and on this basis decides to be his queen.
$(Vm_1)(Af_2)$	(c)	(i)	Carota tells Anna not to tell her father about all this.
(H)	(b)	(s)	Letter from Amandus says he tried to be heroic, ran out into forest in despair, but got soaked and a belly-ache. Cannot challenge Carota to duel, since he would be shedding blood, the blood of a glorious poet. Will write epigrams instead.
$(Af_2)(H)$	(c)	f_1	Anna, under influence of Carota, sends letter to Amandus rejecting him since he will never be king.

Chars	World	Functions	

Chapter V

$(Am_1)(Af_2)$	(c)	e (−i)	Anna learns from Zabelthau that Carota is from lowest order of gnomes, which tend vegetables. Anna is not horrified, but delighted; tells father of Carota's realm.
$(Am_1)(Af_2)$	(b)	(i) (s)	Father warns Anna again of this marriage. Performs ritual to protect her from impending evil.
(Af_2)	(b)	−e	Anna looks into tent, and instead of palace, sees puddle, worms. She is now turning into gnome.

Chapter VI

$(H)(Vm_1)$	(c)	e	Amandus believes in greatness of Carota, who told Amandus he was divine poet and offered him post of court poet. Amandus assigns Anna role of unattainable woman, serves as inspiration (like great poets of the past).
$(Vm_1)(H)$ (Am_1)	(b)	(s)	Amandus sings song and inadvertently overcomes Carota, who shrinks to a tiny carrot and disappears in reaction to Amandus' terrible verse. Zabelthau remarks, "What the most profound magic art was unable to achieve, your verses have done!"
$(H)(Af_2)$	(c)	−e (l_1)	Amandus believes Carota is not great, for otherwise he would not have crawled into the ground on hearing his sublime song. Amandus and Anna marry.
$(H)(Af_2)$	d	(l_2)	Anna now never digs or weeds, but has servants do it. Amandus now regards career of poet as silly. They live happily ever after.

Time P

The King's Bride is one of Hoffmann's most brilliant attempts at self-parody. Each of the characters is a parody of one of Hoffmann's major character types. Zabelthau could be a great sage, but his rituals to obtain occult knowledge are ridiculous; Anna could be the inspiration for Amandus, but she does not even have the wit to understand his poor poetry and prefers vegetables to metaphors; Amandus is easily deceived into accepting the villain's duplicity when he offers to make him court poet. He quickly gives up the struggle for creativity and enjoys the comfortable life of the Philistine. The pseudo-spiritual world of the good and the beautiful alternates with the demonic, but both are finally rejected for the world of the Philistine. The hero and heroine occupy a more or less equal number of scenes, because the story is about self-delusion, which includes both the pseudo-poet and the pseudo-muse. Many of the functions which appear in Hoffmann tales become transmogrified because of the ends for which they are employed as well as the manner in which they are carried out.

IV Puškin: THE QUEEN OF SPADES

Characters:

(H)	Germann, son of German who had settled in Russia, and who left him capital sum. Engineer. Had strong passions, but avoided extravagance, gambling. He would not "risk the necessary in the hope of acquiring the superfluous."
(Vm_{1a})	Saint-Germain, mysterious, in touch with occult.
(Vm_{1b})	Čekalinskij, 60, dignified banker at gaming table.
(Vm_2)	Čaplickij, young man to whom Countess tells secret of three cards.
(Vf_1)	Countess, 60 years before great beauty, now faded. Room full of porcelain shepherdesses popular when Mesmer's magnetism was invented.
Pm_{2a}	Tomskij, grandson of Countess, friend of Germann.
Pm_{2b}	Germann's friends
(Af_2)	Lizaveta Ivanovna, poor orphan, ward of countess. Hopes deliverer will come as in romantic novels she reads.

Chars	World	Functions	
Chapter I			
(H), Pm_2	d	a	Card party at Narumov's, officer of Horse Guards.
(H), Pm_2	(c)	f, q	Tomskij tells about his grandmother, inadvertently arousing side of Germann normally suppressed.
Tomskij's Story			
$(Vf_1)(Vm_{1a})$	(c)	f_1, o_1	Countess gambles and loses. Turns to St.-Germain for help. He reveals secret of card game to her. She wins.

Chars	World	Functions	
$(H), Pm_{2b}$		n	Germann's friends say it was luck, cards were marked. Germann says it is a fairy tale.
$(Vm_2), (Vf_1)$	(c)	$o_1, f_1,$ i, j	Čaplickij needs money; Countess reveals secret as long as he promises never to gamble again. He obeys the interdiction and wins.

Chapter II

Chars	World	Functions	
(Vf_1)	(c)	e	The Countess' "ritual" — her toilette. Pot of rouge, hair pins, all to cover up faded beauty.
(H)	(c)	$f_1, -f, f_1$	Germann begins to appear across from Lizaveta's window every day. He is not ready to become Countess' lover to obtain her secret. First he rejects this temptation to sin, but one day finds himself in front of her house. "It was *as though* some supernatural force drew him there" (italics mine).

Chapter III

Chars	World	Functions	
$(H)(Am_2)$	(b)	(l_1)	Lizaveta receives love letter from Germann copied from German novel. She did not know German, so was delighted. They begin correspondence. Soon his letters are original, written from his unbridled imagination. Lizaveta accepts them eagerly, sets up rendezvous.
(H)	(c)	f_1	When Countess and Lizaveta leave for ball, Germann sneaks into house, goes to Countess' room instead of Lizaveta's.
$(H)(Vf_1)$	(c)	$-e$	Another "ritual" — undressing of Countess. Closely-cropped head under wig, puffy feet, body swaying to and fro.
$(H)(Vf_1)$	(c)	(o)	Germann asks for her occult knowledge. Countess replies it was a joke. Germann appeals to her as wife, beloved, mother.
$(H)(Vf_1)$	(c)	f_1	Germann threatens her with gun, but she dies first.

Chars	World	Functions	
Chapter IV			
(Af_2), Pm_2	(c)	q	At ball Tomskij tells Lizaveta that Germann has profile of a Napoleon, soul of a Mephistopheles, and must have three crimes on his conscience. It was small talk, but it deeply affected her.
$(H)(Af_2)$	(c)	−e	Germann goes to Lizaveta and tells her he is cause of Countess' death. Lizaveta now realizes that she was his pawn, all he wanted was money. Germann feels no pricks of conscience, and sneaks out of house safely.
Chapter V			
$(H)(Vf_1)$	(c)	f_1	Countess' funeral. Priest says the Countess is awaiting the midnight coming of the bridegroom. As Germann looks into coffin, it *seems to him* she winks at him.
(H)	d	n	Germann goes to inn and drinks a lot of wine, which excites his imagination.
$(H)(Vf_1)$	(c)	i,o	Countess appears to him. Says she has come against her will, but tells him: three, seven, ace will win. He must never play again and must marry Lizaveta.
$(H)(Vf_1)$	(c)		Idea of winning drives out guilt over old woman. Has vision of 3 blossoming like flower, 7 taking form of Gothic portal, ace becoming spiders.
$(H)(Vm_{1b})$	(c)	f_1	Germann goes to Čekalinskij's gaming table, wins first two nights.
(H)	(c)	$-i, o_2$	Germann does not marry Lizaveta, but goes third night and turns up Queen of Spades; sees it as Countess.
Conclusion			
(H)	(c)	h_2	Germann in madhouse, keeps repeating: "3, 7, ace! 3, 7, queen!"
(Af_2)	d	d_2	Lizaveta marries civil servant, son of Countess' former steward. She is now bringing up a poor relative.
Pm_{2a}	d	d_2	Tomskij marries Princess Pauline; has been promoted to captain.

Time: D DP P IP P IP P F

Like Hoffmann's own parodies, *The Queen of Spades* includes the basic Hoffmann characters and functions, but they are transmogrified and ridiculed. Through this ridicule, however, the typical devices of the Hoffman tale are laid bare and we become more aware of the elements and patterns that are inherent to it.

As in many Hoffman tales, three worlds are presented, an everyday Philistine world that does not believe in the irrational, and a spiritual world that is divided into the demonic and the realm of the good and the beautiful. Characters like Tomskij and Germann's friends prefer a world where realistic explanations exist for seemingly irrational events. The Countess and St. Germain are seemingly in touch with the demonic, while Lizaveta lives in a sentimentalized version of the realm of the good and the beautiful based on the popular romances she has read. Puškin's work resembles Hoffmann's tales of the fantastic rather than the marvelous. The narrator consistently provides realistic motivation for irrational events, yet adds such phrases as "probably" and "it seemed to him," which couch the event in either the irrational or the real.[28]

Like many of Hoffmann's heroes, Germann is provided with choice, but prefers to blame his interest in the demonic on outside forces. His goal is not to be a great poet like Anselmus, but to gain great wealth out of sheer greed. He courts the seeming muse, but not for inspiration for great poetry, but to gain access to the Countess. His epistles, his "great creations," are either copies of German passages in novels or letters reflecting an "unfettered imagination" rather than the controlled "emotion recollected in tranquility" which is necessary for great art. Like the Philistines in Hoffmann's tales, when Hermann turns to the spiritual, he achieves only the demonic and never attains the heights of the realm of the good and the beautiful. He resembles Hoffmann's hero Nathaniel in "The Sandman" who also can be seen as a parody of the true creator. His poetry is superficial, he does not have the greatness to cope with the irrational forces that have been unleashed within him, and he goes mad.

Lizaveta is a deceptive agent of the world of the good and the beautiful. Like Serpentina, she reveals the path for the hero to take so he may come in contact with the irrational world, but does so inadvertently by providing him access to the house for their rendezvous. She fails to have the insight to judge the superficiality of Germann's powers, but believes them to exist because she wishes to live out the role of the heroines in the sentimental novels she is reading. As others have pointed out, her motives for her relationship with Germann were just as egotistical as his. She was using him to extract herself from her situation as ward. She is happy to marry the civil servant at the end and lead a life of comfortable, Philistine security. Her fate is not all that different from Hoffmann's parody figure Anna in "The King's Bride."

The Countess is a deceptive villain on many counts. If she did have access to occult knowledge, it was only because she asked someone else for it once; it was not something she acquired through her own rituals and contact with demonic agents. In comparison with the witch in *The Golden Pot*, she is weak and pathetic, an outmoded old lady rather than a grand, demonic witch. Her "rituals" are mainly of the toilette, using cosmetics to hide ugly reality. The juxtaposition of the porcelain shepherdesses and Mesmer's magnetism[29] shows that the occult is merely another bauble, another fashion of the time not to be taken too seriously.

The functions also are similar to the Hoffmann tale. There is courtship of a muse, but it turns out to be the courtship of a sentimental Philistine instead. There is temptation of the hero, but the Countess rejects his desire to sin rather than accepting it initially. There is combat with the Countess, but it is so that the hero can sin rather than overcome sin. He does not even murder her properly — she dies of fright instead! There is deception, but when Lizaveta finds out what Germann is really like, she does not pine away in despair, but settles down to a nice, comfortable life with her civil servant husband instead. The madness of Germann is not the result of his contact with the occult so much as guilt over the death of the Countess or frustration for losing so much wealth.

There is a similarity in the way both Puškin and Hoffmann employ time. Like many Hoffmann tales, past, present, and future are interspersed at relevant intervals in the story for the purposes of creating suspense or to provide information at required moments within the structure. The exchange of letters can also be seen as a borrowing from Hoffmann rather than necessarily a parody of the epistolary novel (such as *Clarissa*), for such correspondence between hero and heroine also exists in *The Sandman* and *The King's Bride*. In the latter work it is used to bring out the ridiculous aspect of the hero and heroine just as it is in Puškin's story. There is also the same continuous alternation of the various worlds as in the Hoffmann tale.

On the one hand, Charles Passage is correct when he notes the seriousness and probing of the human dilemma in *The Queen of Spades*. However, the work does have a comic, grotesque side as well. With the schemata of the Hoffmann tale as background, we can see how Puškin masterfully parodied the Kunst-märchen tradition. He has taken specific character types and typical actions and exaggerated and inverted them for purposes of parody. Yet, as Shaw has pointed out in discussions of *Evgenij Onegin*, we laugh at Evgenij and Tat'jana as literary parodies of the Sentimental and Byronic tradition, but we sympathize with them as characters who strive to be larger than life, but whose human limitations prevent them from succeeding.[30] The same can be said for Germann and Lizaveta. This is perhaps one of the elements wherein Puškin's greatness lies.[31]

NOTES

1. For the sociological approach, see G. A. Gukovskij, *Puškin i problemy realisti-českogo stilja* (Moscow: Gosizdat, 1957). For psychological interpretations see Mixail Geršenzon, *Mudrost' Puškina* (Moscow: Knogoizdatel'stvo pistalej, 1919) and M. and A. Schwartz, "The Queen of Spades: A Psychoanalytic Interpretation," *Texas Studies in Literature and Language*, XVIII (1975), 275-288; philosophical analysis occurs in Paul Debreczeny, "Poetry and Prose in 'The Queen of Spades'," *Canadian/American Slavic Studies*, 11 (1977), 91-113 and Lotman, Ju. M., "Tema kart i kartočnoj igry v russkoj literature načale XIX veka," *Trudy po znakovym sistemam*, VII (Tartu: Tartuskij gos. univ., 1975), 122-142. V. V. Vinogradov discusses formalistic aspects of the story in "Stil' 'Pikovoj damy'," *Puškin: Vremennik*, II (Moscow-Leningrad: Akademija nauk, 1936), 74-148.

2. See V. Propp, *Morphology of the Folktale*, 2nd ed. (Austin: U. of Texas Press, 1968). An example of the modification of Propp's morphology for a different set of texts is Tzvetan Todorov, *Grammaire du Décaméron* (The Hague: Mouton, 1969), and Étienne Souriau, *Les deux cent mille situations dramatiques* (Paris: Flammarion, 1950).

3. For critics on possible sources for *The Queen of Spades*, see D. M. Šarypkin, "Vokrug 'Pikovoj damy'," *Vremennik Puškinskoj komissii 1972*, 128-138; D. Jakubovič, "Literaturnyj fon' 'Pikovoj damy'," *Literaturnyj sovremennik*, I (1935), 206-212; and Richard Gregg, "Balzac and the Women in 'The Queen of Spades'," *Slavic East European Journal*, X (1966), 279-283.

4. Bžoza, Galina, "Dualizm immamentoj mirovozzrenčeskoj sistemy *Pikovoj damy* A. Puškina," *O poetyce Aleksandra Puszkina* (Poznan: UAM, 1975), 83-100.

5. Andrej Kodjak, " 'The Queen of Spades' in the Context of the Faust Legend," *Alexander Pushkin* (New York: N.Y. Univ. Press, 1976), 87-119.

6. V. Vinogradov, *Stil' Puškina* (Moscow: Xudlit, 1941), 587.

7. John Bayley, *Pushkin* (Cambridge: Cambridge Univ. Press, 1971), 322.

8. Bayley, 320.

9. A. B. Botnikova, "Puškin i Gofman," *Puškin i ego sovremenniki* (vyp. zp. Leningr. ped. in-ta im. A. I. Gercena, No. 434, 1970), 158.

10. Charles Passage, *The Russian Hoffmannists* (The Hague: Mouton, 1963), 132.

11. Norman Ingham, *E.T.A. Hoffmann's Reception in Russia* (Wurzburg: Jal Verlag, 1974) Colloquium Slavicum VI, 138.

12. Xodasevič, V., *Stat'i o russkoj poèzii* (Letchworth, England: Pridau Prideaux Press, 1971; 1st ed. 1922), 89.

13. J. T. Shaw, "The Conclusion of Pushkin's 'Queen of Spades'," *Studies in Russian and Polish Literature in Honor of Waclaw Lednicki* (The Hague: Mouton, 1962), 126.

14. J. Douglas-Clayton, *Parody and Burlesque in the Work of A. S. Pushkin* (Ann Arbor: Xerox Microfilms, 1976), 207. He also sees similarities between the story and Stendahl's *The Red and the Black*.

15. Izmajlov, N. V., "Fantastičeskaja povest'," *Russkaja povest' XIX veka*, ed. B. S. Mejlax (Leningrad: Nauka, 1973), 134.

16. It contained the twelve-volume French translation of Hoffmann by Loeve-Veimars (Paris, 1829-33), a two-volume collection, *Contes et fantasies* (1834) in Loeve-Veimars' translation, and this translator's biography of Hoffmann (1833). It also contained "L'elixir du diable" translated by Jean Cohen (Paris, 1829).

17. Cited by Ingham, 118.

18. Puškin told this tale at a social gathering. The tale was written down by Vladimir Titov, who checked details later with Puškin and then published it under the pseudonym Tit Kosmokratov (see Passage, 116). In this tale the existence of the irrational is accepted.

19. Both Ingham and Passage find it difficult to point to anything particularly Hoffmannesque in the work.

20. Tzvetan Todorov, *The Fantastic*, trans. R. Howard (Ithica, N.Y.: Cornell University Press, 1973), 41.

21. Wolfgang Kayser, *The Grotesque in Art and Literature*, trans. Ulrich Weinstein (N.Y.: McGraw-Hill Book Co. 1963), 184.

22. Arthur Gloor, *E.T.A. Hoffmann* (Zurich: Arthur Gloor, 1947), 24.

23. Cited by Harvey Hewett-Thayer, *Hoffmann: Author of Tales* (Princeton: Princeton Univ. Press, 1948), 185.

24. Hewett-Thayer, 168.

25. Kenneth Negus, *E.T.A. Hoffmann's Other World* (Philadelphia: U. of Penn. Press, 1965), 162. Many of these ideas are similar to those espoused later by Carl Jung. He proposed an animus side to the mind which is rational and the anima which is intuitive and irrational. There must be a harmony between the two, or energy will build up and the suppressed aspect will explode into disorder and chaos.

26. Hewett-Thayer, 376.

27. Propp, 21.

28. Dostoevsky remarks on the superb rendering of the ambiguity here in his advice to an author:
Let this be a fantastic tale, but the fantastic in art has its limits and rules. The fantastic must be contiguous with the real, so you must *almost* believe it. Puškin, having given us almost all forms of art, wrote *The Queen of Spades* – the height of the art of the fantastic. And you believe that Germann really had a vision, conformable with his world view, and yet at the end of the story, that is, having finished reading it, you do not know how to decide: did this vision come from Germann's nature, or is it really one of those visions contiguous to another world of evil spirits hostile to man (i.e. Spiritism and its teachings). This is real art! F. Dostoevsky, *Pis'ma* in *Polnoe sobranie sočinenii*, IV (Moscow: Gosizdat, 1959), 178.

29. M. P. Alekseev, "Puškin i nauka ego vremeni," *Puškin: Issledovanija i materialy* (Moscow-Leningrad: Akademija nauk, 1956), I, 9-126, tries to prove that by Puškin's time magnetism, galvanism, Mesmerism, etc. were proven to be scientifically based and thus do not have associations in the story with the occult. However, while there may be realistic explanations provided for the irrational events that occur, the Countess is associated at least in Germann's mind with the occult and the irrational, and in the literary code of the time Mesmerism and the psychological effect of magnetism were set in opposition to "scientific" medicinal remedies. The interest in Mesmerism at the end of the eighteenth century is interpreted by most scholars as a change in intellectual climate from rationalism to irrationalism. It was analogous to a similar change in Greece at the end of the second century BC (See E. P. Dodd, *The Greeks and the Irrational*, Berkeley: U. of California, 1951, 246).

30. Personal communication.

31. I would like to thank Stephen Gross for suggesting the application of Proppian analysis to the problem of literary parody and for the many discussions we had about this article.

OLD POKROVSKIJ: TECHNIQUE AND MEANING
IN A CHARACTER FOIL IN DOSTOEVSKIJ'S *POOR FOLK*

Gary Rosenshield, University of Wisconsin

One of the most interesting aspects about Dostoevskij's first novel, *Poor Folk* (*Bednye ljudi*), is its remarkable similarity to the later novels — especially *Crime and Punishment* — in its method of characterization. The protagonist of *Poor Folk*, Makar Devuškin, like Raskol'nikov, is surrounded by a number of lesser figures whose main function it is to increase our understanding of the hero as well as the major themes of the novel. In *Poor Folk* these character foils — or "doubles" as they are called in the later works — have, with the exception of Akakij Akakievič of "The Overcoat" (*Šinel'*), received relatively little scholarly attention. This is especially true of Old (*starik*) Pokrovskij, who plays an important role in the characterization of Devuškin, in the plot, and in Dostoevskij's polemic with Gogol' over the true nature of the *činovnik*, the unprepossessing hero of the writers of the Natural School.[1]

Pokrovskij is introduced relatively early in the novel, appearing as a figure in Varen'ka's written account of her life at the house of the procuress, Anna Fedorovna. She writes Devuškin that Pokrovskij was the father of a poor, young, consumptive student named Peten'ka, with whom she had fallen in love. It is not difficult to conclude, however, that Peten'ka's real father was not Pokrovskij, but Bykov, a coarse and dissolute country squire, who seduced Peten'ka's mother and then arranged her marriage to Pokrovskij. (It would seem that even at that time Pokrovskij was in dire financial straits.) Despite the circumstances of the marriage, Pokrovskij came to love his new wife deeply. She dies, however, only four years later. Soon after her death, Pokrovskij remarried, this time, taking as his wife an ill-tempered merchant woman, to whom he is still married at the time of the events which Varen'ka recounts.

Since Pokrovskij plays a rather insignificant role in Varen'ka's own story, it would seem that Dostoevskij introduces him essentially to establish a foil to Devuškin as early in the work as possible. Dostoevskij's technique here is not unusual. It differs little from his presentation, for example, of Marmeladov as a foil to Raskol'nikov in the second chapter of *Crime and Punishment*.

As with all the other foils in the novel, Pokrovskij's resemblance to Devuškin is striking. It is evident from the beginning that Devuškin and Pokrovskij are small, timid, passive men with little or no self-confidence or self-esteem. They view their social insignificance as an indication of their worth as human beings. Shabbily dressed, clumsy, and ill at ease in company, they both cut rather ridiculous figures. Most of the similarities between Pokrovskij and Devuškin, however, become evident only as the plot fully unwinds: Devuškin does not start off as a "double" of Pokrovskij, but is gradually transformed into one only as his financial and emotional condition progressively worsens. Towards the end of the novel, for example, Devuškin finds himself as destitute and as dependent on others as was Pokrovskij; his clothes deteriorate significantly; and he is in danger of losing his job for the very same reason — drunkenness — that Pokrovskij was dismissed from his position. Although Devuškin is not presented as an inveterate drunkard — which Pokrovskij is — towards the end he is drinking rather heavily. And after Varen'ka leaves him, the reader is to assume that he will, like Puškin's stationmaster, who is a foil both to Devuškin and Pokrovskij, take to drink and die of a broken heart.

It is not at all accidental that Devuškin takes on the characteristics and enters into the situation of Pokrovskij; it is, in fact, essential to the plot. For one of Pokrovskij's main functions in the novel is accurately to foreshadow Devuškin's fate.[2] Since the two characters are similar and since Pokrovskij's story occurs so early in the novel, the reader cannot help projecting Pokrovskij's fate onto Devuškin. Pokrovskij's story, then, serves as a main component of the novel's dramatic irony.

Pokrovskij's story, despite Varen'ka's reticences, is quite simple. When Varen'ka first meets him, he is still without work of any kind; his second wife beats him; he is frequently drunk; and most important for Pokrovskij himself, he is an embarrassment to his son. Then his fortune seems suddenly to change. He is able, with Varen'ka's assistance, to purchase for his son's birthday a set of the complete works of Puškin, whom he knows his son greatly admires. For several weeks preceding the birthday, in anticipation of giving the gift, he makes a serious effort to reduce his drinking; and on the big day itself, he is so pleased with himself that he simply cannot sit still. With the giving of the present, not only has he risen in his own esteem, but he has also gained the respect of the person whom he adores and idolizes. However, shortly thereafter, disaster strikes: Peten'ka dies of consumption. Grief-stricken and distraught, Pokrovskij follows the coffin bearing his son to the cemetery. We know that he will not — that he cannot — sustain the loss; he will take to drink again and die of a broken heart. Pokrovskij's story is essentially made up of three motifs; first, there is a long period of misfortune; then, a sudden reversal, which brings about almost undreamed-of happiness; and shortly afterwards — the final misfortune, the loss of the loved one and the implied death, or at least the psychological destruction, of the bereaved.

Devuškin's story generally follows the same line of development. At the beginning of the novel, we find Devuškin happy, even optimistic (a stage roughly corresponding to the time when Pokrovskij was still living with his first wife). He has moved in order to be near his beloved Varen'ka. It is early spring, and the weather is particularly fine. But as time goes by Devuškin's condition; both material and mental, gets progressively worse; so that by the end of summer, he is destitute and in complete despair. He has taken to drink, and on several occasions has been so intoxicated that he has had to be carried home by the police. But just at the point where all appears lost, Devuškin receives a gift of a hundred rubles from his superior — a totally unexpected stroke of good fortune. His financial and spiritual problems — so it seems to him — are solved; he can now buy all those material objects that he thinks necessary for maintaining his dignity; and more important, he can once again support Varen'ka. (For the last month or so, in a significant reversal of roles, Varen'ka has, in effect, been supporting Devuškin.) Soon after the good fortune, as we would expect on the basis of Pokrovskij's story, tragedy strikes: Devuškin learns that Varen'ka has made an unalterable decision to marry Bykov and leave Petersburg. The novel ends with Varen'ka, already wed, on her way to Bykov's estate in the country. Like Pokrovskij, Devuškin is bereft of the person who made his life worth living, who restored to him his sense of dignity; like Pokrovskij, Devuškin, it is implied, will not survive his bereavement: he too will die, in sentimental fashion, of a broken heart.

The ways in which Pokrovskij is similar to Devuškin, however, are of much less importance than the ways in which he is different from Devuškin. In Dostoevskij, the similarities of foils are often merely the necessary foundation for exploring the significance of their differences. The nature of these differences and the reasons for developing them are best understood in the context of Dostoevskij's polemic with Gogol''s presentation of Akakij Akakievič in "The Overcoat." It has been argued — and with a good deal of justice — that Devuškin is Dostoevskij's answer to Gogol''s unsympathetic and depreciating portrait of the simple man — in particular, the intellectually limited and downtrodden clerk of the Natural School.[3] Whereas Gogol' portrayed his "hero" as devoid of all positive human traits, almost as a subhuman whose love could not extend beyond his obsession with an overcoat (Gogol''s work is cast in the form of a parody of a sentimental love story), Dostoevskij portrayed the same titular councilor as fully capable of experiencing and expressing the tenderest and most self-sacrificing aspects of sentimental love. Devuškin, that is, the činovnik, was no less a man than those, as Belinskij stated, who lived in the gilded palaces of Petersburg.[4] To present him the way Gogol' had presented Akakij Akakievič, as Devuškin himself argues, is to palm off as real what in fact is a malicious distortion of reality.[5]

But to restore the human being in the činovnik Dostoevskij purposely overstated his case, not as greatly as Gogol' overstated his, but overstated it enough so that Dostoevskij himself must have seen that his position with regard to Devuškin had some of the same weaknesses, as far as characterization is concerned, as Gogol''s presentation of Akakij Akakievič. For if Akakij Akakievič is the clerk stripped of his humanity, an almost allegorical symbol of the negative ideal, then Devuškin is in many ways an idealization of this very same clerk — albeit in the other direction.

This "relative" idealization has been overlooked by critics of the novel. The generally held view is that Devuškin is an Akakij Akakievič except for his great love for Varen'ka.[6] Indeed, like Akakij Akakievič, Devuškin is a copying clerk and titular councilor; he is a small, timid, lonely man, poorly educated and intellectually limited, and he attaches a great deal of importance to material objects, especially clothes. Akakij Akakievič has an obsession with overcoats, Devuškin with boots. But these similarities are, in the final analysis, superficial. The differences between the characters are much greater than the similarities and they go much beyond the difference between Devuškin's love for Varen'ka and Akakij Akakievič's "love" for his overcoat – however great and significant Devuškin's love may be. For love is just one of the spheres in which Devuškin is shown to be considerably different from, even superior to, Akakij Akakievič.

However limited, Devuškin is a complete human being: there are many sides to his personality. He is what E. M. Forster has called a round character. Devuškin, for example, spends time with his fellow lodgers; he occasionally goes to the theater; he reads, and, of course, has a passion for writing. At times he even engages in a little freethinking. (Akakij Akakievič is barely capable of rational thought.) Devuškin also has a sense of humor. Whereas Akakij Akakievič is parsimonious and makes sacrifices only in his own interest, Devuškin is generous and self-sacrificing: he is able to transcend the limits of the self. Furthermore, and perhaps most important, he is compassionate: his heart is wrung when he sees young children begging in the street and he gives his last twenty kopecks to the destitute Gorškov. It is true that he is uneducated, but he is often aware of his own ignorance and is not content with it; he aspires to better things.

But if, as said above, Devuškin was in several ways almost as much a "distortion" of the real clerk as Gogol''s Akakij Akakievič; if, in matters of the greatest importance, Devuškin was almost as much a positive as Akakij Akakievič was a negative ideal, could Devuškin be used as an example to prove that even the humblest of men have the potential for expressing and experiencing the same depths of love as the greatest of sentimental lovers? It would seem that Dostoevskij clearly needed another character to somehow right the balance, that is, a realistic corrective to Akakij Akakievič, and ultimately to Devuškin himself, a clerk who loves deeply, but not quite with the heart of a Grandison.

Such a type was never to be in Dostoevskij's arsenal. His solution to this dilemma, a solution more conducive to his talents, was to resort, paradoxically, to still another extreme type: Pokrovskij. Pokrovskij is actually a fusion of many of the negative traits of Devuškin taken to their logical conclusions and of traits absent in Devuškin, but prominent in Akakij Akakievič. The result of this fusion is not only an extreme character but a character who is in many ways closer to Akakij Akakievič than to Devuškin.

Devuškin, for example, is poorly dressed, but not nearly so poorly dressed as Pokrovskij. Devuškin may walk around with holes in his shoes, but it is doubtful whether he would report to the office with a hat like Pokrovskij's, crumpled, full of holes, and with a torn brim. Devuškin's demeanor is undignified, but again Pokrovskij's is still more so: he is extremely awkward and clumsy, and his gestures are a constant source of amusement to Varen'ka and her cousin Saša, who often cannot contain their laughter in his presence.

Devuškin's position, it is true, is an insignificant one; he is a mere copying clerk. But at least he has a job and has had one for nearly thirty years. Pokrovskij, on the other hand, is unemployed and has not worked for the longest time. Once, like Devuškin, he had a place in the civil service, but it was the lowest, most insignificant of positions − that is, much lower even than Devuškin's. And, as stated before, he lost this post as a result of drunkenness. As regards drunkenness, we have seen that although Devuškin at times can drink heavily, he is not an inveterate drunkard like Pokrovskij.

Like Devuškin, Pokrovskij is timid, but he is much more like Akakij Akakievič in this respect, for he is timid to the point where there seems to be nothing he does not fear: he is afraid of Anna Fedorovna, of his wife, even of his own son. When he comes to visit Peten'ka, he tiptoes in as much from fear, as from his concern not to be a nuisance. He is scrunched up as though he were trying to hide or protect himself from life, just as Akakij Akakievič tries to protect himself with his overcoat. In contrast to Devuškin, who takes to freethinking at the time of his worst troubles, Pokrovskij passively accepts his situation − in word and deed.[7] His response to misfortune, like Akakij Akakievič's, is resignation: he meekly puts up with the ridicule and insults of his fellow men, the intimidation of his wife, and the disrespect of his own son.

But perhaps the area in which Pokrovskij and Devuškin differ most significantly is speech. The clerks of the Natural School − Akakij Akakievič is a perfect example − were, as a rule, remarkably inarticulate. Devuškin is actually the most important exception to the tradition. Though his language is shot through with saccharine diminutives, bureaucratic jargon, and other infelicities, it is nevertheless quite expressive; it turns out to be an effective instrument for expressing the sentiments of the heart.[8] Pokrovskij is more in the *činovnik* tradition. Like Akakij Akakievič he can hardly speak. As Varen'ka says, he was not born with the gift of words. And when he does speak he makes little sense, asking ridiculous, meaningless questions, and generally creating a nuisance out of himself. Pokrovskij, then, just like Akakij Akakievič, plays an important role in emphasizing the ways in which Devuškin transcends the poor clerk of the Natural School.

It is evident, I think, from the above comparisons that it is not Devuškin, but Pokrovskij who is the real double of Akakij Akakievič in *Poor Folk*. But, as we might expect of Dostoevskij, he is a double with a difference: Pokrovskij is an Akakij Akakievič who can experience great love, a love, moreover, which in its essential features is no way inferior to Devuškin's.[9] What is especially important, however, is that Pokrovskij, in contrast to Devuškin, differs from Akakij Akakievič only in his capacity for love. Whereas Devuškin's human qualities are revealed not only in his love for Varen'ka but also in his compassion, humor, and willingness to sacrifice himself for others, it is love alone that raises Pokrovskij from the status of an automaton — that is, from being an Akakij Akakievič — to a true human being. For Pokrovskij is essentially an Akakij Akakievič humanized by his great love for a boy who is not even his own son, but the son of his wife's seducer. Varen'ka is often given to exaggeration, but her assessment of Pokrovskij's love can be taken to be Dostoevskij's as well: "The only evidence in him of human feeling was his boundless love for his son" (p. 54).[10]

In placing Pokrovskij in this role Dostoevskij was obviously taking great artistic risks. For whereas the reader may accept the fact that a man like Devuškin, though he be only a clerk, can possess a great capacity for love, he will certainly find it more difficult to accept such a capacity in a close copy of Akakij Akakievič. On the other hand, if Dostoevskij can make the reader accept Pokrovskij's love as believable — and I think he does — then he can effect a remarkable *tour de force*. For if Pokrovskij, obviously a worse case (his situation, is, after all, in some respects much more wretched than Akakij Akakievič's) can love so deeply, then all clerks — in fact, all men, no matter how humble they may be — can, or at least have the potential to, do likewise. In Pokrovskij, then, Dostoevskij strikes a blow at the very heart of Gogol''s pessimistic view of man, not only as it is presented in "The Overcoat" but as it is presented in Gogol''s entire opus.

There are several other significant differences between Devuškin and Pokrovskij that deserve special attention. These have to do with the difference between Devuškin's and Pokrovskij's love. As has been pointed out by Victor Terras, Devuškin, in most of his endeavors, must be considered a dismal failure.[11] He is unable to protect Varen'ka either physically or financially. He cuts a ridiculous figure as a lover and his behavior before His Excellency is so abject that Belinskij was positively horrified by it. However, with regard to matters of the heart, Devuškin is, relatively speaking, an idealization of the *činovnik*. Yet he is only a "relative ideal," for great though his love may be, it is by no means presented as perfect. One of the most important functions of Pokrovskij is to shed light on the less positive aspects of Devuškin's love. As we shall see, Pokrovskij's love for his son, Peten'ka, provides a touchstone for evaluating Devuškin's relationship with Varen'ka.

The shortcoming that most mars Devuškin's relationship with Varen'ka is his inordinate concern with what other people think of him, a concern which manifests itself in his preoccupation with his appearance and reputation. Devuškin believes that he is what people think he is and that his dignity as a man is directly dependent upon, even identical to, his reputation. He not only worries about his reputation, he is to a large degree ruled by what he thinks others might be thinking of him. Appearances for him become the essential reality. In contrast to Akakij Akakievič, who needed an overcoat for protection against the

Petersburg cold, Devuškin needs boots to protect him from the malicious tongues of his fellow workers.[12]

The poor, as Dostoevskij often showed, are hypersensitive, and it is perhaps understandable why Devuškin values his reputation so dearly. Where Dostoevskij, however, undercuts Devuškin's position is Devuškin's frequent equation of reputation and human dignity. In the depths of despair Devuškin talks about the Greek sages going around barefoot and begins to question whether money and good clothes make the man, but this period of freethinking is short-lived. He reveals more of his true self in the following passages:

> What will my enemies with their evil tongues say, when I go out without an overcoat? You know you even wear an overcoat for others, and perhaps you even wear boots for others as well. Boots, in such a case, my dear, my darling, are necessary to maintain one's dignity and good name; if one has holes in one's boots, both are lost — believe me, my dear, believe my long experience; listen to an old man who knows the world and people, and not to scribblers and hacks. (76.)

> Well, as everything is over now and things are little by little returning to normal, I would like to say this to you, my dear: you are concerned with what people will think of me, to which I hasten to inform you, Varvara Alekseevna, that my reputation (*ambicija*) is dearer to me than anything in the world. Because of it, while I have been relating to you my misfortunes and all these disorders, I must tell you that no one from my office knows anything yet, and no one will, so that they all will treat me with the same respect (*uvaženie*). I fear only one thing: gossip. (65.)

Dostoevskij would not be so harsh on Devuškin on this point if Devuškin had not already shown that he is capable of understanding the difference between reputation and human dignity, and if he had not let it affect, and rather adversely, his relationship with Varen'ka.[13]

The adverse effect that Devuškin's concern for reputation has on his relationship with Varen'ka is most dramatically shown in Devuškin's failure to visit Varen'ka as often as he should. Varen'ka continually urges him to visit her and as often as possible, but Devuškin finds excuses for not coming: he is afraid that he will be seen going to her apartment and that people will start talking. Therefore, he confines his visits, for the most part, to evenings after dark. But since it gets dark so late in Petersburg in the summer, when most of the action in the novel takes place, he visits very infrequently. It must be admitted that Devuškin is concerned with Varen'ka's reputation, too. But it is evident from the letters that the main reason he does not visit more often is the fear that he will appear ridiculous to others and will set tongues wagging – that is, the reputation that will suffer most is his own.[14]

Pokrovskij's attitude toward the views of others is quite different from Devuškin's, and as we shall see, it has significance for our understanding of Devuškin's love for Varen'ka. Dostoevskij treats this difference in attitude in terms of appearance, more specifically, in terms of clothes. Pokrovskij, like Devuškin, is not indifferent to clothes. On his son's birthday, for example, he arrives wearing a new waistcoat (bought with his son's help), a decently mended swallow-tailed coat, and a new pair of boots (bought for him by his wife.) He is noticeably pleased with his appearance. But he is pleased only because he knows that dressing presentably is pleasing to his son. What is important to him is how he appears to Peten'ka, not how he appears to others. He is concerned with the impression he makes on Varen'ka and Saša because he loves them almost as much as he does Peten'ka. On the other hand, he does not seem to care at all what Anna Fedorovna thinks of him although it is in his interest to appease her, for she can prevent him from seeing his son. Devuškin, by contrast, often seems more concerned with the impression he makes on others than with the impression he makes on Varen'ka. When he takes to drink and has been conducting himself rather improperly, for which Varen'ka severely reproaches him, Devuškin seems less concerned with Varen'ka's reprimand than with what his fellow workers at the office might say if they learned of his most recent behavior. Indeed, at times, he acts as though his reputation, as he himself says, really were dearer to him than anything in the world – dearer, in fact, than Varen'ka herself.

What is most important, however, is that in contrast to Devuškin Pokrovskij does not let his ridiculous appearance, the fact that he is laughed at, stop him from visiting his son as often as possible. And he would visit him every day if his son permitted; for clearly the visits are the happiest moments in his life. We have seen that with Varen'ka and Devuškin the exact opposite situation obtains. It is Varen'ka who urges Devuškin to come more often and Devuškin who searches for excuses not to come. What is more, Dostoevskij presents Pokrovskij's too frequent visits much less negatively than Devuškin's too infrequent ones. Pokrovskij, as Varen'ka admits, could be a regular nuisance, and Peten'ka was forced to limit his visits so he could attend to his studies. Dostoevskij, however, excuses Pokrovskij's behavior because it is motivated from great love. But if Pokrovskij persists in visiting Peten'ka even though he often disturbs him, Devuškin persists in not visiting Varen'ka precisely when she most needs him. Varen'ka is by nature sickly and given to bouts of depression; moreover, her situation is desperate. Devuškin's letters are important to her, but they are often an inadequate substitute for his physical presence. Varen'ka frequently tells Devuškin how much better she feels after he has visited. In fact, one gets the impression that she would like Devuškin to write her less and visit her more.

Thus, at least in his failure to be with Varen'ka when she needs him most, Devuškin is clearly derelict in his duty as a lover — one might even say sentimental lover. For it seems that Dostoevskij has structured the amatory situation in such a way that the reader is compelled to evaluate Devuškin's failure in sentimental terms. Whereas the typical sentimental lover does everything in his power to be with his beloved, but is prevented from doing so by external circumstances, Devuškin can visit any time he wishes, but of his own free will chooses to stay away. Even in sentimental terms, then, Devuškin is far from the ideal lover.

Pokrovskij's behavior after the death of his son provides Dostoevskij with another means for showing how Devuškin's love falls short of the sentimental ideal. The pathetic image of Pokrovskij trailing after his son's coffin determines to a significant extent what Devuškin writes and thinks about himself, if not what he actually does. Devuškin never explicitly identifies himself with Pokrovskij (he is probably as reluctant, understandably, to see himself in Pokrovskij as he was to see himself in Akakij Akakievič), but the letter of July 1 shows that, at least unconsciously, Pokrovskij is very much on his mind. In this letter, Devuškin, having learned that Varen'ka is considering a position as a governess, urges her to dismiss the very idea, arguing that not only will she be unable to survive in the midst of strangers, but that he, too, will not survive if she leaves him. Devuškin threatens to put an end to himself if she abandons him: "I've grown accustomed to you, my dear. And just what will come of it [Varen'ka's leaving]. I'll go to the Neva and put an end to it all. Yes, really that's how it will be, Varen'ka; what will I do without you! Oh, my darling, Varen'ka! It's plain that you want a drayman to take me to Volkovo [Cemetery], you want some bedraggled old beggar woman, all alone, to follow my coffin, you want them to cover me with sand, to go away, and leave me all alone!" (58.) Devuškin is obviously trying to use every means at his disposal to persuade Varen'ka to stay. For here he very cleverly alludes to her extremely sentimental description of Pokrovskij's following the coffin of his dead son to the cemetery:

(Varen'ka's letter)	(Devuškin's letter)
Na uglu ulicy uvjazalas' s nim vmeste provožat' grob kakaja-to niščaja staruxa. (45.)	Xočetsja, vidno, vam, čtoby menja lomovoj izvozčik na Volkovo svez; čtoby kakaja-nibud' tam niščaja staruxa-pošlepnica odna moj grob provožala. . . (58.)

The correspondence is purposely inexact, for here Devuškin is attempting to play the parts of both Pokrovskij and his son in order to elicit as much sympathy from Varen'ka as possible. His main idea is that if Varen'ka leaves she will be as dead for him as Peten'ka was for Pokrovskij. But it would be unrealistic — and in very poor taste — to picture himself accompanying Varen'ka's coffin to the cemetery as Pokrovskij accompanied Peten'ka's. Moreover, since Devuškin at this moment sees himself as the one who will suffer most from Varen'ka's departure, he imagines that he, like Peten'ka, is in the coffin; for losing Varen'ka is for him tantamount to death. Nevertheless, Pokrovskij is at the heart of the description. Pokrovskij's following the coffin, accompanied by an old beggar woman, and his implied death afterwards, are compressed into Devuškin's being in the coffin, accompanied by the same old beggar woman. Devuškin could devise no more effective way of telling Varen'ka how much he loves her and how much she means to him than by saying that his love for her is as great as Pokrovskij's love for his son, and that if she leaves him he will end up just as Pokrovskij did.

But when Varen'ka finally leaves, Devuškin does not follow her, as Pokrovskij followed his son — and as, by the way, Samson Vyrin followed Dunja to Petersburg.[15] In fact, he is prosaically incapacitated by a cold on the day of her departure and cannot go out. Nor does he throw himself, as he had threatened, under the carriage taking Varen'ka away to the country. Having cast himself in the sentimental role of Pokrovskij, Devuškin finds that this is another role to which he is unequal. Even from his own sentimental point of view, Devuškin has been plainly outdone by his foil, Old Pokrovskij.

It should be emphasized, however, that Dostoevskij shows the shortcomings of Devuškin's love not to demonstrate that his love is intrinsically deficient. If anything it is, on the whole, idealized. It is for a very different reason that Dostoevskij uses Pokrovskij to point out the weak points in Devuškin's relationship with Varen'ka: the need for verisimilitude. To make Devuškin perfect as a lover, especially given his situation and background, would in the end detract from, if not destroy, his credibility as a character. Devuškin is more successful as a three-dimensional character because of it. In fact the extremeness of Pokrovskij — and for that matter all of Devuškin's foils in the novel — makes Devuškin, by contrast, seem not so unusual at all. In this way Dostoevskij is able to demonstrate that Devuškin's compassion, humor, and generosity as well as his love are not the exclusive property of his hero, but exist potentially in all but the very humblest of men.

NOTES

1. To my knowledge, there are no studies devoted to the characterization in *Poor Folk* of Gorškov, Samson Vyrin, or Pokrovskij. Of the work done on Pokrovskij, the best is that of V. V. Vinogradov, "Škola sentimental'nogo naturalizma: Roman Dostoevskogo 'Bednye ljudi' na fone literaturnoj èvoljucii 40-x godov," in his *Èvoljucija russkogo naturalizma: Gogol' i Dostoevskij* (Leningrad: Academia, 1929), 351-55, 375-76. For an excellent discussion of the Natural School, see Vinogradov's "Škola sentimental'nogo naturalizma" and his *Gogol' i natural'naja škola* (Leningrad: Obrazovanie, 1925). For another interesting, but quite different approach, see A. G. Cejtlin, *Povesti o bednom činovnike Dostoevskogo: K istorii odnogo sjužeta* (Moscow, 1923).

2. Vinogradov − "Škola sentimental'nogo naturalizma," 375-76 − notes that Pokrovskij is used to foreshadow Devuškin's tragic fate, and leaves the subject at that. Vinogradov is echoed on this point by N. S. Trubetzkoy, *Dostoevskij als Künstler* (The Hague: Mouton, 1964), 33; Donald Fanger, *Dostoevsky and Romantic Realism,* (Cambridge: Harvard Univ. Press, 1965), 153-55. The Soviets view Pokrovskij as a social variation of Devuškin. His function in the novel, they hold, is to give the reader a more complete picture of urban poverty under Nicholas I. See, for example, V. I. Ètov, *Dostoevskij: Očerk tvorčestva* (Moscow: Prosveščenie, 1968), 67; G. M. Fridlender, "Primečanija," in F. M. Dostoevskij, *Polnoe sobranie sočinenij* (30 vols; Leningrad: Nauka, 1972-), I, 468. The text of *Poor Folk* is from the above edition of Dostoevskij's works. Hereafter in the notes it will be cited as *PSS*. Translations from this edition are mine; page numbers will appear in the text.

3. Konstantin Mochulsky, *Dostoevsky: His Life and Work,* tr. Michael A. Minihan (Princeton: Princeton Univ. Press, 1967), 29-32.

4. V. G. Belinskij, "Peterburgskij sbornik," in *F. M. Dostoevskij v russkoj kritike,* ed. A. P. Belkin (Moscow: GIXL, 1956), 16.

5. See *PSS,* 62-63.

6. Victor Terras, "Problems of Human Existence in the Works of the Young Dosto-evsky," *Slavic Review,* 23 (1964), 84, concludes: "In his love for Varenka, Devushkin is no worse a man than Werther; but when it comes to facing a superior or to measuring the value of a pair of shoes, he is no better than a Bashmachkin." Devuškin's other good personality traits have been noted (for example, Mochulsky, 32; Terras, 85), but the criticism of the novel has not yet come to terms with the significance of these traits for the characterization and thematics of the novel.

7. Devuškin's latent rebelliousness has often been noted. It was first discussed in detail by N. A. Dobroljubov, "Zabitye ljudi," in *Dostoevskij v russkoj kritike,* 71-73, 86. For the most recent treatment of the subject, see W. J. Leatherbarrow, "The Rag with Ambition: The Problem of Self-Will in Dostoevsky's 'Bednyye lyudi' and 'Dvoynik,'" *Modern Language Review,* 68 (1973), 607-18.

8. Devuškin's language is examined in detail by Vinogradov, "Realizm i razvitie russkogo literaturnogo jazyka" in his *O jazyke xudožestvennoj literatury* (Moscow: Goslit-izdat, 1959), 477-93. See also Trubetzkoy, 39-40.

9. Belinskij, 16, found Pokrovskij's love moving, but it reminded him nevertheless of the timid love of a dog for its master. Belinskij most admired the pathetic aspects of Pokrovskij's characterization.

10. Pokrovskij has often been likened to Balzac's Père Goriot. The similarity had been noted as early as 1846 by Apollon Grigor'ev. Goriot is consumed by his love for his children; he lives entirely for them; and in the end, dies because of them. The differences, however, are at least as great as the similarities. Pokrovskij does not have Goriot's abilities

and strengths. He also has nothing to sacrifice. In fact, he is partially supported by his son, who, rather than taking advantage of his father — which is unimaginable for a number of reasons — even attempts to reform him. Devuškin is probably much more like Goriot than Pokrovskij. Like Goriot, Devuškin makes sacrifices which are not in the end properly appreciated by the ones for whom they were made. For a brief discussion of Goriot and Pokrovskij, see Dominique Arban, *Les Années d'apprentissage de Feodor Dostoievskij* (Paris: Payot, 1968), 259.

11. Terras, 80-84.

12. For an examination of the themes of dignity and reputation in *Poor Folk,* see Terras, 81-84.

13. See, for example, Devuškin's statements on the Greek sages (81) and on the relationship between wealth and moral worth (85-86).

14. Of course, Devuškin's failure to visit Varen'ka as often as he should can be viewed as a device used to motivate the exchange of letters of persons who live so close to each other. Dostoevskij, however, motivates Devuškin's infrequent visits so well psychologically that it is impossible to determine whether the device was motivated by the characterization of the hero or the characterization of the hero by the device. Here Dostoevskij seems to have it both ways.

15. For Puškin's sympathetic treatment of Vyrin, see J. Thomas Shaw, "Puškin's 'The Stationmaster' and the New Testament Parable," *Slavic and East European Journal,* 21 (1977), 3-29.

THE PASSIONATE PAGE: "FIRST LOVE" AND "THE LITTLE HERO"

Pierre R. Hart, Louisiana State University at Baton Rouge

Shortly after publication of the revised version of Dostoevskij's "The Little Hero," a second work of fiction appeared, in April of 1860, which also centered about the recall of sexual awakening. Turgenev's "First Love," like the story of his contemporary, describes the emotional trauma experienced by a naive boy as a consequence of his involvement with a young woman. Both stories employ the same symbolic imagery to heighten the distinction between childhood sentiment and adult passion, invoking notions relating to the Age of Chivalry, and the coincidence of particulars is sufficient to raise the question of Dostoevskij's influence on Turgenev.[1] Of greater interest, however, is the comparison of the two works as realizations of a common theme. The product of distinctly different stages of their authors' evolution, they reflect the relative mastery of psychological portraiture by each author at a particular point in time.

In Dostoevskij's case, it is important to note that his story was actually written shortly after his imprisonment in 1849. It must therefore be regarded as the product of a writer who had yet to undergo the experiences which were of such great consequence for the mature novels. Yet the fact remains that he chose to publish the story in revised form after his return from exile, suggesting that it retained some value in the author's eyes, if only as a retrospective and perhaps nostalgic statement on the idealism of youth. Turgenev, by contrast, was at the height of his career, having demonstrated his talent in a series of novels and short stories during the 1850's. It is the latter group, including *The Correspondence, Jakob Pasynkov,* and *Faust* which, in their exploration of the themes of love and death,[2] establish the basis for the composition of "First Love." Turgenev's story, commonly acknowledged as one of his finest, by virtue of its structural unity and evocative tone, might thus be considered a culminating statement on two of its author's most persistent concerns.

Both authors chose fictional memoirs as their narrative vehicle, describing childhood experience through the double filter of time and imagination. Autobiographical accounts of youth had come into their own during the 1850's, with the publication of Tolstoj's *Childhood* and Aksakov's *The Childhood Years of the Grandchild Bagrov.* To the degree that they offered a record of actual events, they might be regarded as different from Dostoevskij and Turgenev's fiction. Yet, as recent studies of the nature of autobiography have emphasized, imagination plays a substantial role in its composition and, whatever the distinction in particulars, it shares a number of primary features with fiction: "Autobiographies, as much as novels, depend on narration, provide explanations, and insist on the comprehensibility of life."[3] Given this fundamental identity, we might consider the extent to which the two stories contribute to the representation of childhood in Russian prose and, more specifically, their relationship to autobiography.

Judged on the basis of Dostoevskij's early fiction, it is evident that he conceived "The Little Hero" as an experiment in theme and form alike, one of several works subtitled "From Anonymous Notes/Memoirs." Unusually optimistic in tone, the story is devoid of any detail which might invite comparison with events from the author's own life. The narration centers almost exclusively on the Little Hero's experience, with only an occasional judgment offered by the adult narrator as he describes his past. Interestingly, one of the few major changes which Dostoevskij introduced into the 1860 version was the deletion of the adult narrator's garrulous introduction, thereby reducing our awareness of his presence in the work. The total effect is that of a psychological etude, engaging rather than profound and quite unlike the portraits of children to be found in the mature novels.

Turgenev's work occupies a much more central position in his *oeuvre,* convincingly proving his success with the novella as a form for character depiction and development. Unlike the narrator in Dostoevskij's work, Vladimir Petrovič emerges as a distinct personality and his assessment of his own youthful experiences contributes significantly to the story's impact. The author's frequently quoted observation that he lacked the power of imagination and could only work from life holds particular relevance for "First Love." In addition to Turgenev's declaration that he intended the father to be a portrayal of his own parent, recent archival studies have identified the minor poetess Elizaveta Šakovskaja as the model for Zinaida.[4] Circumstantial evidence suggests a factual basis for the illicit affair described in the story although Turgenev's own relationship to the young woman can only be deduced from the fiction.

If "First Love" must nominally be categorized as fiction, it is still true that it resembles Tolstoj and Aksakov's autobiographies more closely than does "The Little Hero." In so doing, its theme of sexual rivalry between father and son acquires an intensity that Dostoevskij's work lacks. Although the aesthetic gain is one which subsequent generations might appreciate, the story's subject matter provoked accusations of bad taste among Turgenev's contemporaries.[5] Such a reaction might well have been expected and could even have motivated the use of a fictional narrative frame.[6] Rather than presenting his reader with an unmediated confession of personal experience, he elected to establish a certain distance by attributing the account to an independent figure. Without denying the contribution of actual events to the story, the reader can reasonably consider "First Love" as a self-sufficient entity, dependent upon internal dynamics for its effects.

Direct comparison of the adult narrators' commentary on their own youthful perceptions helps to illustrate their respective roles. Both boys must contend with adult male rivals but the judgments passed on these men are patently born of subsequent deliberation and experience rather than being the direct transcript of the child's impressions. In the case of "The Little Hero," one of those singled out for such commentary is Madame M.'s husband. Immediately following a description of his physical appearance, the adult narrator makes his presence felt: "He was called a *man of intelligence*. In other circles, a particular sort is thus named who grows fat at the expense of others, who does absolutely nothing, who wants to do absolutely nothing, and whose eternal laziness and indolence has resulted in a piece of fat instead of a heart."[7] The incongruity of this brief diatribe in the midst of the boy's naive account is immediately apparent and its social message does little to advance our appreciation of the personal relationships as the Little Hero initially viewed them.

The analogous example from "First Love," an assessment of the father's character, is also the result of mature reflection but it more effectively complements the observations and experiences of the youth. Vladimir Petrovič remarks that his father had married his mother "in a calculating manner" (*po rasčetu*) and that he had never seen a "more exquisitely calm, self-assured, and controlled" person. At the moment they are offered, these comments may appear gratuitous yet, as we subsequently discover, they help to define the relationship between father and son and, equally importantly, introduce the theme of dominance and subjugation which is at the center of the entire work. Direct confirmation of both the son's judgment and its thematic importance is subsequently provided when his father advises: "Take what you can for yourself and don't surrender yourself to others. . ." (30)

It is, however, important to both stories' effect that the mood of youthful naivete prevails. At an early point each narrator attempts to convey something of the emotional turmoil which he had earlier endured. Vladimir Petrovič admits the impulsive romantic nature of his thoughts and acts, even though it lends a slightly comic touch to the self-portrait. Immediately following the remarks about his father, he offers a brief description of his own character: ". . . my heart ached so sweetly and foolishly. I constantly awaited something which made me tremble, I marvelled at everything and was in a state of readiness. . . I would fall into reverie, become sad and even cry, but through both the tears and sorrow. . . there was the joyous feeling of youthful, surging life." (90) With the possible exception of the term "foolishly" (*smešno*), the adult narrator does not attempt to judge his earlier behavior but simply conveys the prevailing mood of his adolescence.

The narrator's account of the Little Hero's newly developed feelings is remarkably similar even though there is an age difference of six years between the boys: ". . . something incomprehensible to me, a sensation, had already taken control; something which had earlier been unfamiliar and unknown, was rustling in my heart but because of it, my heart flamed and throbbed, as though frightened, and often, an unexpected flush came over my face." (269) This relatively sober judgment is offset by other passages in which that same touch of amusement as was evidenced in "First Love" can be detected.

Because the configurations of characters are different, these attempts at self-portraits exert different influences upon the works in their entirety. Of the individuals depicted in "The Little Hero," only the main character is provided with any indication of psychological complexity. The young adults by whom he is surrounded are simply foils for advancing the action and offer no meaningful alternatives in attitude or behavior. Such is not the case in "First Love," as a consideration of the three central figures makes clear. The father's deliberate, controlled actions contrast with those typical of the young Volodja and are the cause for the latter's admiration if not his envy. Their mutual attraction to Zinaida and the specifics of their respective relationships with her are consistent with their differences in personality. Unlike his father, the narrator confesses that his own early thoughts and feelings held hidden "some half-conscious, shy presentiment of something new, inexpressibly sweet, feminine." (9) By virtue of its tentative nature, this attitude makes Volodja subject to manipulation at the hands of those more experienced in affairs of the heart.

There are several parallels between the stories, that of the boys' involvement with somewhat older, capricious young women being the most striking. A variety of vaguely erotic, sometimes sado-masochistic feelings emerges in the course of their association and neither of the boys is sufficiently experienced to cope with them directly. The Little Hero's dilemma is further complicated by the presence of Madame M., whose madonna-like beauty and composure contrast with the blonde's spirited, if somewhat cruel, behavior. It would appear that Dostoevskij used the heroines of two of Schiller's ballads as his models, posing a choice for the Little Hero in terms of the Code of Chivalry.[8] At the story's outset, the boy contents himself with the role of a submissive page in the service of Madame M. Goaded by the young blonde's taunts, however, he impulsively proves his knightly qualities by riding a spirited horse and is treated in much different manner as a result. As this suggests, his overt action is central to the change in his status. He does not come to a new attitude towards women through reflection; it is thrust upon him by the course of events. Given the fact that he is only eleven, a more deliberate change might well have appeared improbably precocious. At the story's conclusion, the narrator remarks simply that his "first childhood" had ended, without elaborating on his subsequent emotional development.

Zinaida embodies qualities of both the madonna and the temptress, making her one of Turgenev's most interesting women characters. "The possibility of sorrowful and ardent passion," which he had attributed to his very first heroine, Paraša, was of constant concern, in some instances manifesting itself as altruistic sacrifice and in others, as a drive to dominate. Prior to the completion of "First Love" the author's tendency was to represent the two impulses separately although Elena, in *On the Eve,* anticipates the union of opposites that distinguishes Zinaida.[9] This duality is vital to "First Love," justifying the triangular relationship between the two males and the young woman. By turn submissive and domineering, she satisfies each of them as well as finding satisfaction for herself. More than a mere catalyst for Volodja's actions, Zinaida holds the key to Turgenev's definition of adult love relationships and the boy is confronted with her behavior as something totally alien to his own childlike views.

For the greater part of the narration, Volodja is bewildered by Zinaida's attitudes. His own notions about love are quite like those of the Little Hero at the outset, involving self-sacrifice without expectation of reward, as exemplified by the page's devotion to his lady. Dostoevskij had relied upon the transformation of page into knight to symbolize the maturational process, implying that an essentially romantic concept of love could be maintained in adulthood. Turgenev, by contrast, expressed little confidence in such an exalted notion. The love that draws Zinaida and Volodja's father to each other has about it a quality of "selfishness that is redeemed by self-justifying vitality."[10] Rather than sharing and accommodation, it involves struggle that is to the ultimate detriment of both partners. Only the child's innocence prevents recognition of this inescapable fact and the mature narrator, in recounting the events, takes care to preserve this illusion. There is no response from the boy, for example, when Zinaida declares: "No I cannot love those whom I must look down upon. I need the sort of person who might break me. . ." (34)

The initial identification of child and page in both stories merits particular consideration because it marks a common point of departure for the boys' emotional development. At least consciously, the Little Hero prefers that role, readily accepting such a part in a tableau, "The Lady of the Castle and Her Page." When Madame M.'s husband uses the term "cavalier servant" to describe the boy's relationship to his wife, it is vehemently denied. Yet there are several hints of his interest in the recognition accorded a knight even before his wild ride. He imagines himself as a participant in a tourney, flattered by the "timid cry of a single, frightened heart." His fascination with the young blonde's physical attributes also suggests a nascent interest in the type of relationship that would be denied a page. It is the blonde's taunting use of the word "page" which, in fact, impels him to ride the stallion. Whatever worth he had earlier placed in his service to Madame M. is suddenly denied by a desire to prove himself to the young blonde. Impulsive and premature though his action may be, it is consistent with the notion of adolescent developmental processes.

Although Volodja is older and hence, at least in theory, better prepared for the more mature role, he remains a page to the story's conclusion. As a witness to the world of adult passions, he comes to understand it in some degree, yet he appears lamed by this very knowledge. Rather than venturing forth into that world, Volodja holds to his refuge. Zinaida, much like Dostoevskij's blonde, takes the initiative in deciding the roles of her admirers. During one of her conversations with Volodja, she proposes that he accept the designation of page, placing a rose in his buttonhole to signify his new status. As the boy observes, he is still a child in her eyes and this proposal confirms his suspicion. Although he momentarily objects, he assumes the role without discomfort and shows little inclination to change it. There is but one point at which he takes exception to the appelation "page," in a scene which echoes that to be found in the "Little Hero." Zinaida relates the fantasy about herself as a queen, awaiting her lover in the garden, to which Malevskij caustically responds that "Monsieur Voldemar, in his capacity as the Queen's page, ought to hold her train, should she hasten to the garden." (55) Whether Volodja suspects the identity of Zinaida's lover is uncertain but he is, in any case, being asked to stand witness to her liaison with another man. The Little Hero insisted on the title of page in disavowal of any sexual interest; Volodja appears to reject it for the same reasons. Interestingly, Zinaida is also offended by Malevskij's remark and demands that he leave.

To be sure, Volodja occasionally entertains the notion of a more heroic stance, but his actions are of little consequence. The incident which most closely parallels the Little Hero's test develops from a similarly capricious demand by the heroine. Zinaida, catching sight of Volodja on top of a fifteen foot wall, asks that he jump from it as proof of his devotion. Although he immediately complies, losing consciousness as a result, the act does not basically alter their relationship. As soon as he recovers, Zinaida assumes the same imperious attitude as before. Only the boy himself persists in the illusion that Zinaida's momentary concern has signified a change in the terms of their friendship. Reflecting upon the scene, Volodja indulges in the same sort of melodramatic fantasy as the Little Hero had prior to his ride: "I began to imagine how I would save her from the hands of enemies; how, covered with blood, I would drag her out of a dungeon; how I would die at her feet." (48) Noble though his intentions may be, they are immediately forgotten when the boy becomes engrossed in the activities of a large, brightly-colored woodpecker which is climbing a tree!

A second, potentially sterner test of his manly virtues is prompted by Zinaida's presumably imaginary description of the nocturnal rendezvous. Volodja recognizes that there is some truth in her account and finds himself envying the "lucky fellow by the fountain." His first attempt to discover the man's identity is an innocuous one and meets with failure. When Malevskij reminds him that a true page should watch over his mistress day and night, however, he assumes a much more aggressive attitude, seizing a penknife and casting himself in the role of the avenging lover. Thus armed, he discovers his rival's identity and the adult narrator's description of his reaction is noteworthy: "Jealous Othello, ready for murder, was suddenly transformed into a schoolboy." (61) It might, of course, be argued that only the prospect of parricide compels Volodja to abandon the part that he has impulsively assumed. Yet his response is consistent with the whole of his character; it is clear that he is incapable of more than innocuous gestures in imitation of adult passion. Whatever his rival's identity, Volodja would content himself with imaginary acts of vengeance. In the case of "The Little Hero," coming of age is associated with formal proofs of one's maturity; in "First Love," the situation admits of no such solution.

Yet another aspect of the page-knight juxtaposition merits consideration in the comparison of the two texts — that of horsemanship.[11] At an early point in the story, immediately following Volodja's account of a visit to the Zasekins', his father gets up and leaves to saddle his horse. Characterizing him as an "excellent horseman," the narrator adds a detail which, at first glance, seems to contribute little to the total portrait: "He was able, long before Rarey, to break (*ukroščat'*) the wildest horses." (31) Apart from the curious comparison with a nineteenth-century American trainer, there are several fictional parallels, including Vronskij's handling of horses in *Anna Karenina*. More specifically, we might consider the relationship between the man's treatment of horses and women. Turgenev's use of such symbolism anticipates Tolstoj's in that the father's attributes as a horseman are fully consistent with the rest of his personality.[12] The principle of control is one that he extends to every aspect of his life. In "The Little Hero" the boy gains acceptance by riding the unbroken stallion, Tancred, a feat which its owner claims to be worthy of a true Il'ja Muromec. Volodja, by contrast, admires his father's abilities but appears incapable of equalling them. His most explicit comments on the subject come just prior to his witness of the final meeting between Zinaida and his father. Everything about the man's presence in the saddle, consistent with the image of the proud, self-assured individual, makes his loss of control in Zinaida's presence all the more dramatic: "He sat so beautifully and with such casual grace that it seemed the horse beneath him sensed this and was showing him off." (69)

This impression of harmony and effortless control is shattered by the incident which follows. Dismounting from his horse and leaving it in Volodja's care, the father goes by foot to his meeting with Zinaida, taking with him a riding whip, the obvious means of maintaining control over his horse. In a moment of anger he strikes Zinaida with the whip, and the image of the reddened welt which is raised is implanted upon the boy's memory. Volodja is understandably horrified by the blow and specifically asks about the whip after his father's return, even though he had seen him cast it aside. Moreover, he dreams that same night of his father, standing with whip in hand while Zinaida cowers in a corner, the welt visible on her forehead. His dream simply heightens the boy's realization of the strength of adult passion and the subjugating impulse which he has observed in fact. That romantic notion of love characteristic of the page can no longer be sustained. Although Volodja may concede the potential for violence and its acceptance by those who love, the thought is disquieting, and his characterization of such emotion suggests his personal apprehension.

Love looms like "an alien, beautiful, but threatening face which one strives in vain to discern in the dusk. . ." (72) The very combination of threat and appeal in this personification might be taken as emblematic of adult love in Turgenev's fiction. Volodja is atypical only to the degree that he experiences it vicariously rather than directly.

In addition to its effect upon the boy's appreciation of love's ambiguities, the incident causes a change in Volodja's attitude toward his father. Terrible though the whip lash may be, it helps to dispel the image of remoteness which the man had succeeded in cultivating with his son. Previously, Volodja had experienced only frustration in his efforts at friendship but now, at least, the facade has cracked. As they return home on horseback, Volodja notes for the first time "the great tenderness and compassion" that his father's stern features can express. Although there is no explicit discussion of the incident between them, the father's subsequent letter suggests that he is aware of his son's knowledge. Begun on the morning of his fatal stroke, it contains a warning which can best be understood in the context of his own actions: "Fear woman's love, fear that happiness, that poison." (72) The narrator does not comment on either the fact of his father's death or on the contents of the letter but his juxtaposition of the two is noteworthy. As is so frequently the case in Turgenev's fiction, love has destructive consequences, as the father's use of the word "poison" (*otrava*) would suggest.

Both in sequential relation and function, the father's death invites comparison with analogous events in Turgenev's novels. In the latter genre, ". . . some incompatibility between hero and heroine. . . prevents any further development in their relationship. . ." and subsequent to the exposure of that flaw, the narration ". . . takes the form of a protracted conclusion or epilogue." (Freeborn, 55) In "First Love," internal dissonance is of greater importance, the father's realization of his own incapacity to maintain control over his emotions almost certainly contributing to his demise. Structurally, this event marks the conclusion to the description of the boy's experience, being followed by an epilogue offered from the perspective of the twenty-year old student. The fact that Volodja himself remains to reflect upon the implications of earlier events distinguishes the work from those in which the main figure dies. In order to appreciate Vladimir Petrovič's total development, the relationship of attitudes expressed in the epilogue should be related to those in the story proper.

It has been postulated that "First Love" is Turgenev's attempt to trace the psychological origins of the superfluous man to the trauma of early love.[13] The factual basis for such a conclusion is tenuous since we know only that Vladimir Petrovič is a bachelor of about forty at the time of his narration. In addition, his relative effectiveness as a member of Russian society remains undefined. Yet the combination of his experience and the deaths of Zinaida and his father appear to have made him a tentative participant in the game of life. Zinaida's loss in particular prompts him to reflect on the general issue of youth's unsuspecting profligacy and enthusiasm in the face of impending doom. The delicate balance between life's vital forces and the oblivion of death suddenly tips to the latter's advantage at that moment: "And perhaps the whole secret of your [youth's] charm lies not in the possibility of doing everything but in the possibility of thinking that you will do everything, it lies in the fact that you waste your strength, which you do not know how to use for any other purpose. . ." (75) There is a bittersweet quality about these thoughts, a retrospective recognition of futility which is still untinged by regret.

In terms of his own psychological development, Vladimir Petrovič recognizes the inadequacy of that romantic ideal by which his earlier life was governed. Having witnessed the passion, as well as the potential for destruction inherent in adult relationships, however, he is equally unable to expose himself to those perils. Thus constrained, Vladimir Petrovič might well be considered one of those superfluous men who, paralyzed by the whole of life, can only occupy themselves with memories of an innocence lost.

NOTES

1. The possibility of such influence is mentioned, without further elaboration, in the notes for "The Little Hero," in F. M. Dostoevskij, *Polnoe sobranie sočinenij v tridcati tomax,* (Leningrad: Nauka, 1972), II, 502.

2. Richard Freeborn, *Turgenev: The Novelist's Novelist* (London: Oxford University Press, 1960), 43, points to these and other stories written during the 1850's as the basis for Turgenev's development of the thematic interrelationship in the novella.

3. Patricia M. Spacks, *Imagining a Self* (Cambridge: Harvard University Press, 1976), 18.

4. For a decent discussion of the factual basis for this story, see N. Černov, "Povest' I. S. Turgeneva 'Pervaja ljubov" i ee real'nye istočniki," *Voprosy literatury,* 1973, No. 9, 225-41.

5. In response to this criticism, Turgenev justified his choice on the grounds that it had been given to him "in its entirety by life itself." See Turgenev's letter to E. E. Lambert of February 18, 1861. I. S. Turgenev, *Polnoe sobranie sočinenij i pisem,* (Moscow-Leningrad: Nauka, 1962), B, IV, 201. All subsequent references to Turgenev's works are taken from Section A of this edition and are indicated within parentheses at the appropriate point in the text.

6. Ralph E. Matlaw, "Turgenev's Novels and *Fathers and Sons,*" in Ivan Turgenev, *Fathers and Sons,* Ralph E. Matlaw, ed., Norton Critical Edition (New York: W. W. Norton, 1966), 272, stresses the separate function and personality of the adult narrator in this story: "The achievement of this story lies in that it is not merely a perfect rendition of 'first love,' but that it simultaneously paints and characterizes the middle-aged bachelor who is the narrator. The narrator now understands many things beyond his comprehension then. But in the very process of narration he also indicates the profound and lasting effect of this experience and how it shaped him into the personality he now is."

7. F. M. Dostoevskij, *Polnoe sobranie sočinenij v tridcati tomax,* II, 275. All subsequent references to this story are taken from this edition and indicated in parentheses at the appropriate point in the text.

8. For a discussion of the contribution of these ballads to Dostoevskij's story, see Pierre R. Hart, "Schillerean Themes in Dostoevskij's 'Malen'kij geroj'," *Slavic and East European Journal,* XV (Fall 1971), 305-15.

9. Eva Kagan-Kans, *Hamlet and Don Quixote: Turgenev's Ambivalent Vision* (The Hague: Mouton, 1979), 41-55, traces the evolution of Turgenev's heroine from the seemingly pure maiden of the early works to the mature, predatory woman. As she observes, the potential for both impulses is present in all of his females.

10. D. S. Mirsky, *A History of Russian Literature from Its Beginnings to 1900* (New York: Alfred Knopf, 1958), 203.

11. Judith Oloskey Mills, "Theme and Symbol in 'First Love'," *Slavic and East European Journal,* XV (Winter 1971), 438-39, discusses this imagery as it relates to maturity and masculinity.

12. Barbara Hardy, *The Appropriate Form* (London: Athlone Press, 1964), 179-80, argues that Tolstoj is successful because the symbolism of the race scene does not overwhelm the scene's figurative contribution to the novel's total effect: "It is part of the natural flow of events, and symbolic only in the way in which events are symbolic to life, in their typicality which is only part of their nature and function." Something similar might be said for the significance of horseback riding in "First Love."

13. Mills, "Theme and Symbol in 'First Love'," suggests such an interpretation.

ANTON LAVRENT'EVIČ G-V: THE NARRATOR AS RE-CREATOR IN DOSTOEVSKIJ'S *THE POSSESSED*

Gene Fitzgerald, University of Utah

Literary theorists from Henry James to Wayne Booth point out that narrative point of view in any work is contingent on the author who chooses the narrative mode which he feels will be most effective in transmitting his work's meaning. Further, most critics also insist that once the narrative is decided, the author must maintain a consistent point of view in order to insure the novel's realistic illusion.[1] It is on the issue of narrative inconsistency that many critics, both Western and Soviet, castigate Dostoevskij and his novel, *The Possessed,* a view with which we disagree.

Dostoevskij's choice of narrative mode in *The Possessed* corresponds in many ways to Norman Friedman's category, the " 'I' as witness": a witness-narrator who is a "character in his own right within the story itself, more or less involved in the action, more or less acquainted with its chief personages, who speaks to the reader in the first person."[2] Friedman also defines the "legitimate" boundaries of this narrative frame which the author must observe to maintain a consistent point of view: the author surrenders "his omniscience altogether regarding the other characters involved and has chosen to allow his witness to tell the reader only what he as observer may legitimately discover."[3] The reader is limited to the witness-narrator's perceptions, thoughts, and feelings. However, Friedman asserts that, "what the witness may legitimately transmit to the reader is not as restricted as may at first appear: he can talk to the various people within the story and can get their views on matters of concern; particularly he can have interviews with the protagonist himself; and finally he can secure letters, diaries, and other writings which may offer glimpses of the mental states of others." Finally, "at the utmost limit of his tether," the witness-narrator can infer the thoughts and feelings of other characters.[4]

Anton Lavrent'evič G-v, Dostoevskij's witness-narrator in *The Possessed,* manifests all the qualities Friedman ascribes to the " 'I' as witness" point of view, utilizing all the "legitimate" means available to him, conversations with characters, quotes from letters, eyewitness accounts and inferential judgements of others' mental states, to describe the novel's actions and personages. Yet Dostoevskij allows his narrator to move beyond Friedman's "legitimate" boundaries: Anton Lavrent'evič presents scenes, conversations, and, at times, characters' thoughts that are realistically inaccessible to his "human" self without giving the reader any obvious clues to his authority for such information. And often Soviet and Western critics, in the manner of Friedman's criticism of Samuel Butler for wandering "uncertainly beyond his limits in *The Way for All*

Flesh," allowing his witness-narrator to transmit "too frequently" characters' thoughts without giving the reader a "clue whatever as to his authority for such information," castigate Dostoevskij for allowing his witness-narrator similar liberties.[5]

Although, perhaps, an inconsistent point of view may not necessarily destroy a novel's illusion of reality, in my opinion, Dostoevskij considers a consistent perspective essential in *The Possessed*. This novel, based so closely on actual events, is considered by some critics and Dostoevskij himself as an attempt to present the "truth of Russian contemporary social reality."[6] To this end Dostoevskij chose to present the novel's events through a witness-narrator and character within the novel. Despite D. S. Lixačev's assertion that "it is not important to Dostoevskij to create full-fledged, sharply delineated characters as narrators," and insistence that the narrator in *The Possessed* is "not actually a narrator but rather two points of view... about whom one must forget to a certain degree,"[7] it is clear from the *Notebooks* to *The Possessed* that Dostoevskij not only consciously chose the eyewitness point of view but also expends considerable effort to explain the narrator's plausible authority for information which would be difficult for him to obtain:

> And altogether, whenever I [the narrator] am giving an account of conversations which took place between just two persons, don't pay any attention to this... Either I have positive facts, or I am, perhaps, *inventing* them myself, but in any case, I can assure you that everything is true.[8]

Although this narrative self-vindication does not appear in the novel proper it does reveal Dostoevskij's concern with presenting a plausible, "realistic" witness-narrator since he suggests the dimension of creative invention in the narrator's character and thus makes him a "full-fledged" personage who can legitimately present scenes which he did not witness. Moreover, if Dostoevskij were interested only in developing two different points of view, he could have done so as effectively through other narrative modes which do not necessitate creating a witness-narrator about whom the reader "must forget to a certain degree."[9]

Yet, critics are insistent that, in the novel proper, Anton Lavrent'evič G-v moves beyond his legitimate boundaries. He constantly draws attention to his restricted "human" limitations and then blithely presents private, isolated scenes and conversations which are realistically beyond his knowledge. It seems that either Dostoevskij consciously abuses the limits of his chosen narrative mode, or, as many Soviet critics assert, his artistic talent is inadequate to present his "false" ideas and the narrative contradictions illustrate his "ideological shortcomings."[10] However, we will assert a third alternative, that he presents a plausible witness-narrator who is also an authorial figure in his own right.

The suggestion in the *Notebooks* that the narrator can invent scenes based on his re-creative and inferential abilities adds a significant dimension to the " 'I' as witness" narrative frame. In such a case, an author not only surrenders his omniscient point of view by imbuing his narrator with certain authorial skills, he also surrenders some aspects of his "authorship" as the narrator is given the responsibility to choose the novel's structure, the material to be included in the novel, and the manner of presentation of that material. The *Notebooks* to *The Possessed* again indicate that Dostoevskij's narrator wields such authorial control:

> The system which I [the narrator] have adopted is that of a *Chronicle*. Thus, for instance, Nečaev enters. Here, what his face looks like will be given, and what kind of an impression he made on me.

> *Chroniclers's Comment* [*ot sebja*] : Earlier it was impossible to write a novel here in Russia, but now with publicity (but it is *my* opinion that because of the new order, too), the most romantic *échevelées* stories are possible.[11]

First, these quotes re-emphasize our point that Dostoevskij is concerned with creating a distinct, independent character as a narrator. He emphatically attributes thoughts to the narrator who, as an "I," theorizes on literary matters as independently as Stavrogin will later discuss Christian morality. Indeed, throughout the notebooks Dostoevskij often disappears behind an authorial "I" which must be attributed to the narrator. In many of the notes which are made by an "author" describing Liputin's imagination or commenting on Nečaev's naiveté, it is clear that it is the narrator, not Dostoevskij himself, talking.[12] Second, the narrator is shown fulfilling an authorial role by deciding on his own novelistic "system" of a "chronicle," and discussing the literary problem of point of view in presenting "Nečaev's" character. Finally, he theorizes on the problem of producing literary works in his present-day Russia. Clearly, the narrator of the notebooks is characterized by his literary sensibilities and concern with and control over the structure and point of view of his literary effort.

As we shift our focus away from the notebooks to the text of the novel itself, we must note that V. A. Tunimanov in his fine descriptive study of the narrative in *The Possessed,* also, rather reluctantly, suggests that the narrator must become at times "a creator" who invents scenes and conversations, "and through his imagination fills in the 'lacunae' of his chronicle."[13] Although we agree with Tunimanov, our approach to the narrator's creative abilities differs substantially. Since Tunimanov treats the witness-narrator within traditional boundaries similar to those outlined by Friedman, he is almost apologetic when he suggests the narrator is a creator and he develops the notion no further.[14] That such authorial creativity and manipulation of the text is a plausible inherent characteristic of the witness-narrator generally and of Anton Lavrent'evič G-v specifically will be shown through an examination of his narrative manner: his arrangement of the novel's events (the *sjužet*), his manipulation of perspective, and finally his method of "re-creating" scenes and characters through a conscious repetition of descriptive epithets and evaluations. Thus it is our point that Anton Lavrent'evič invents isolated conversations and scenes, but not as an extraordinary and occasional occurrence, but rather as a "realistic" aspect of his total authorial control of the work.

Franz Stanzel in his work on novelistic narrative situations points out that all first-person narrators appear in their novels as an "experiencing self" and a "narrating self." The narrator as "experiencing self" is a character located contemporaneous to the plot's events and characters who participate in the novel's action; the narrator as "narrating self" is a character located after the novel's events are concluded who describes the action after the fact.[15] This dual appearance affords the narrator complete freedom to manipulate his temporal point of view between an "experiencing" perspective — descriptions limited to eyewitness accounts of the events as they occur without knowledge of later events — and a "narrating" point of view — descriptions of events after the fact with total knowledge of all that has happened. However, in all works in which witness-narrators emphasize that they have composed their works after the novel's conclusion (rather than maintaining a running diary of events), only the "narrating" perspective realistically exists. Whatever perspective a narrator uses to depict characters and events, he chooses it from the perspective of his "narrating self" as he interpolates his experienced historical "raw material" into an "artistically" contrived work. In essence, the work is totally controlled by the narrator's "narrating self." Anton Lavrent'evič fits this narrative frame almost perfectly. He constantly draws attention to the fact that "now that everything is over and I am writing my chronicle,. . . I will endeavor to describe. . . my chronicle, writing. . . with complete knowledge of the circumstances and presenting them as they have now been revealed and explained."[16] Yet, as critics almost universally point out, much of *The Possessed* is narrated "without any time perspective,"[17] that is, from the narrator's "experiencing" perspective. Although this assessment is certainly true, we wish to emphasize that whenever the "experiencing" perspective is used, it is at the choice of the narrator's "narrating self," and is an indication of his ability to control and manipulate the narrative point of view.

The Russian Formalists' important distinction between a novel's *fabula* and *sjužet* provides a basic starting point for critical discussions of an author's structuring of his literary work. In general terms a work's *fabula* is the chronological or chronological-causal sequence into which the reader may reassemble a novel's motifs; it may be viewed as the "raw material" that the author compositionally "deforms" and thus re-contextualizes in constructing his work. The *sjužet*, in contrast, is the actual arrangement and articulation of these narrative motifs in the finished work as their order and interrelation was finally decided on by the author.[18] As we have seen in the notebooks, the narrator consciously chooses as his *sjužet* a chronological ordering of the events into a chronicle, an arrangement which the narrator realizes in the final text. Anton Lavrent'evič refers to his work as a chronology/chronicle no less than nine times in the course of the narrative.[19] A close examination of the novel reveals that the narrator does indeed present the events in a strictly chronological sequence, beginning with a presentation of Stepan Trofimovič's, Varvara Petrovna's, Stavrogin's and Petr Stepanovič's past covering some twenty years, then of episodes just prior to the novel's "fictive present" (events in Switzerland, Stepan Trofimovič's letters to Petr Stepanovič, among other things) which occur from May through July, and finally, the events of the novel proper (the "fictive present")[20] which begin with Liza's, among others', arrival in "our town" on the last Friday in August and culminate in a precise hourly (at times a minute by minute) account of the two days before Šatov's murder and Petr Stepanovič's escape which take place in the first week in October. Stepan Trofimovič's "escape" and death occur in the same time period but are related subsequently.[21] Even though such a strict chronological disposition of the events comes dangerously close to the Formalists' definition of *fabula,* it is, nevertheless, the novel's *sjužet,* chosen and articulated by the work's "author," that is, in this case, Anton Lavrent'evič. As Meir Sternberg points out, it is perfectly plausible for a restricted narrator to "arrange his 'story stuff' in retrospect into the proper chronological order so as to give us at an early stage the benefit of the discoveries that he himself, owing to his human and personal limitations, made much later."[22] Thus the narrator in *The Possessed,* writing from his "narrating" perspective, constructs his own "artistic" chronological *sjužet* from the confusing and haphazard events that he learned in a variety of ways at different times. In so doing he demonstrates his control of the novel's structure and characterizes himself as a figure with authorial traits.

Anton Lavrent'evič G-v's use of his "narrating" perspective to re-contextualize the "historical" events into a chronology and his "experiencing" position to relate those same events without a time perspective is echoed in his manner of character portraiture. In both instances the final form is controlled by the narrator's "narrating self" who willfully manipulates his point of view, often pretending to possess only limited knowledge of events and at other times presenting "facts" as they ultimately became known to him. The narrator's perspectival manipulation is most apparent in his depiction of Stepan Trofimovič and we will limit our discussion here to that characterization.

From the novel's onset it is clear that the narrator intends to present an ironic and ridiculing portrait of Stepan Trofimovič. To achieve his ironic tone he carefully manipulates his point of view to juxtapose Stepan Trofimovič's view of himself (and his conduct which reflects that view), which the narrator pretends to believe and "sincerely" describes from his "experiencing" perspective, to the narrator's perception of him after the completion of all the events which he presents from his "narrating" perspective.[23] His portrayal of Stepan Trofimovič as an important "civic" figure who has been exiled for his dangerous liberal ideas is typical. Beginning from his "experiencing" point of view the narrator declares that Stepan Trofimovič was as famous as Belinskij, Granovskij, Gercen, and other revolutionary thinkers, but because of subversive activities his career was cut short, "owing, so to speak, to a 'vortex of combined curcumstances.' " (8) Abruptly, the narrator switches his point of view and continues the portrayal from his "narrating" perspective:

> And would you believe it? It turned out later that there had been no "vortex" and even no "circumstances"... I learned just a few days ago... that Stepan Trofimovič had been living... in our province not as an exile... and had not even been under police supervision. Such is the force of imagination. (8)

The narrator clearly manipulates his perspective to subjectively ridicule and portray Stepan Trofimovič. Of course, the only valid perspective here is from the "narrating self," as the narrator merely pretends to believe in Stepan Trofimovič's self-image of political activist and exile. After all Anton Lavrent'evič is fully aware of the "true" situation at the time he composes the description; he chooses, however, to shift his perspectives from "experiencing" to "narrating" and through the resultant incongruous views create irony and shape Stepan Trofimovič's character. By the conscious "creative" manipulation of his narrative stance, the narrator also demonstrates his "authorial" control of the presentation of the novel.

Such examples of the narrator's shifting perspective abound in the novel and one other example should suffice to demonstrate his personal direction of the novel's narrative. Again the narrator refers to the "circumstances" that caused Stepan Trofimovič to abandon his career stating from his "experiencing" point of view that a letter "which contained an account of some sort of 'circumstances' " had been intercepted and because of the information in the letter "someone had demanded an explanation from him." Again the narrator shifts to his "narrating" perspective and assures us that he is "fully convinced now" that Stepan Trofimovič had only needed to give "the necessary explanation" and he could have continued his career as a lecturer. Continuing from his "narrating" perspective the narrator asserts that "if the whole truth is to be told the actual cause for the change in Stepan Trofimovič's career was the very delicate proposition which had been made before and then renewed by Varvara Petrovna..." (9-10) Curiously, the narrator seems to contradict and qualify even his apparently "true" assessments made from his "narrating" perspective, here, specifically, his assertion that Stepan Trofimovič's "vortex of circumstances" never existed. The narrator now considers that Stepan Trofimovič did record some liberal thoughts in a letter which was intercepted and for which he was called to account. However, the narrator, considering the episode a trifling matter, attempts to reveal the "whole truth" (apparently the "vortex of circumstances" is a lesser "truth") and asserts that Stepan Trofimovič's decision to change careers was mainly based on Varvara Petrovna's offer of employment. Anton Lavrent'evič's changing perception of the "whole truth" only serves to underscore our point that he exhibits authorial talent in artistically creating and presenting Stepan Trofimovič's character by juxtaposing his different perspectives (both of which are relative truths).[24]

Finally, the narrator's creative imprint is placed on the novel through his widespread use of recurrent epithets and images. Thus, for example, he describes Mar'ja Timofeevna from a first hand observation as "painfully emaciated" (boleznenno-xudoščavuju), wearing an "old dark calico dress" (temnoe staren'koe sitcevoe plat'e); she has a "long neck" (dlinnoju šeej) and her "hair is twisted into a knot on the nape of her neck" (svernutymi na zatylke v uzelok); she "wears powder" (belitsja) and "rouge" (rumjanitsja). (114) Shortly after, the narrator presents an "invented" description of Mar'ja Timofeevna as she arrives at the town's cathedral. At the time the narrator is at Varvara Petrovna's and can not be an eyewitness to the event. His descriptive details are drawn from his previous depiction as he points out that she is "painfully thin" (boleznenno-xuda), "powdered" (nabelena) and "rouged" (narumjanena), with a "long neck" (dlinnoju šeej), wearing an "old dark dress" (staren'kom temnom plat'e), with her "hair tied up into a tiny knot on the nape of her neck" (podvjazannymi v krošečnyj uzelok na zatylke). (122) Clearly, the narrator's repetition of so many exact descriptive details indicates he not only can present characters but he also can consciously create them.

Many such recurrent images appear in connection with the depiction of Stepan Trofimovič. For example, the narrator comments that Stepan Trofimovič is "very handsome" even at age "fifty-three." (19) Later inferring Stepan Trofimovič's thoughts, the narrator states that Stepan Trofimovič felt that he was fascinating to Varvara Petrovna "as a handsome man." (53) Then Varvara Petrovna declares to Dar'ja Pavlovna in a private conversation that Stepan Trofimovič is "still a handsome man" (56) and shortly thereafter insists to Stepan Trofimovič in another isolated conversation, "You are a handsome man and you know it yourself." (61) A similar recurrence of images is found in connection with Stepan Trofimovič's intention to leave Varvara Petrovna and live independent of her. Early in the novel Stepan Trofimovič tells the narrator that he has the strength "to take my bag — my beggar's bag" and leave, perhaps "to end my life as a tutor in a merchant's family or die of hunger by a fence!" (73) Towards the middle of the novel Stepan Trofimovič tells Varvara Petrovna in a private conversation (the narrator is on his way to visit Semen Jakovlevič at the time) that "I will take my sack, my beggar's sack," and leave "to end my life as a tutor in a merchant's family or die somewhere of hunger by a fence." (266) Finally, at the novel's end, the narrator presents the travelling Stepan Trofimovič's thoughts as he asks himself where he is going: "To search for ce

marchand? But what *marchand*? " (480) Shortly, in answer to a peasant's query
why he is going to Xatovo, Stepan Trofimovič replies, "I am going to see a
certain merchant." (484)

The repetitive imagery is also found in connection with Petr Stepanovič. On
Petr Stepanovič's return, the narrator refers to him as the "gentleman who
suddenly dropped from the sky." (148) Later, in a private conversation with
Stavrogin, Petr Stepanovič refers to himself as "neither stupid nor wise, quite
ungifted and I've fallen from the moon as sensible people here say." (175)[25] In
the same conversation he repeats the image twice more: "But they have forgiven
me everything, because, in the first place, I have fallen from the moon"; (176)
"Everyone has already given up on me; 'he has abilities,' they say, 'but he has
fallen from the moon.'" (179)

In all these examples one perceives a pattern of repetition that indicates the
narrator's conscious structuring of his "novel." He first relates a scene or action
in which he personally participates, thus remaining within the "legitimate"
framework of his point of view. Then, by using the same descriptive epithets,
opinions, and evaluations the narrator "re-creates" isolated private scenes and
characters consistent with his earlier observations. The frequency of these verbal
repetitions and the narrator's obvious personal involvement in the descriptions
indicate his conscious manipulation of the text and style. Indeed, at times the
narrator reveals with a certain bravado that he is the novel's controlling force.
Perhaps the clearest example of the narrator's "baring the device" is found in the
description of Mar'ja Timofeevna's paper rose in the "cathedral scene" which we
have already referred to. Re-creating the scene after the fact, the narrator
chooses to describe Mar'ja Timofeevna from an "objective" eyewitness point of
view, that is, as if he were a stranger who had never met and did not recognize
Mar'ja Timofeevna. Thus the narrator never identifies Mar'ja Timofeevna by
name but rather refers to her as "a certain lady," "a strange, unusual creature,"
or simply, "the woman." However, suddenly the narrator breaks the pretense of
his "objective" point of view and observes that in the woman's hair "there was
inserted only a single artificial rose of the sort. . . that was exactly like those
which I had noticed in a corner under the icons when I was sitting at Mar'ja
Timofeevna's." (122) Then again removing his own subjective comments the
narrator reverts to his objective point of view and describes Mar'ja Timofeevna as
the "strange, unusual creature, the woman with the paper rose on her head" who
suddenly knelt before Varvara Petrovna. (123) In this passage the narrator's
manipulation of his point of view and personal involvement is so obvious that
one must consider it not only the narrator's intent but also his wish to display
his "authorial" ability to the reader, to show that it is he who controls the text
of his "chronicle." By having the narrator blatantly "bare the device" of his
authorial creativity, Dostoevskij broadens the eyewitness narrative frame to
include a witness-narrator-authorial figure who creates his own chronicle and

thus can move beyond his limited eyewitness point of view and plausibly re-create isolated scenes.

This scene contains all the "artistic" aspects that we have chosen to demonstrate the narrator's control of the chronicle presentation and will therefore serve as a summary of our argument. First, the narrator strictly adheres to the chronological *sjužet,* using his "narrating" perspective to place the scene, the details of which he learned later, in its correct chronological sequence, and deciding, in the course of the narrative, that he "must go back an hour and describe in detail the extraordinary event which happened with Varvara Petrovna at the cathedral." (121) Second, he manipulates his point of view and subjective distance from the scene in the most undisguised manner, as we have already discussed. Finally, he uses repetitive descriptive epithets taken from his eyewitness observations to re-create Mar'ja Timofeevna's description. These three narrative aspects serve to emphasize our contention that the narrator is also an author and re-creator of his own chronicle-novel. Thus Dostoevskij creates a witness-narrator who can maintain a consistent point of view and present isolated scenes, conversations, and even inner thoughts. At the same time Dostoevskij carefully creates a full-fledged, realistically "human" character as narrator.

While it is important to demonstrate that Anton Lavrent'evič G-v is a "realistic" witness-narrator, perhaps more significant are the reasons for Dostoevskij's choice of this narrative mode. Inasmuch as an author chooses his narrative point of view as a means to achieve certain effects and transmit the meaning of his novelistic world to the reader most effectively, it behooves us to examine Dostoevskij's purpose in writing the novel. A thorough examination of this problem would extend this essay to an unconscionable length; however, I feel some attempt to provide a satisfactory answer to the query is in order.

One of Dostoevskij's primary concerns in *The Possessed* is to portray a world ruled by the "beast" of the apocalypse, a thought which he projects in the notebooks: "The Apocalypse: Try to realize that the beast means nothing but a world which has deserted its faith, reason reduced to its own resources, after it has rejected, on the basis of science, any chance of immediate communion with God. . ."[26] Later Dostoevskij clarifies that "morality and faith are the same thing,"[27] indicating that in his understanding, the apocalyptic world rejects faith and thus morality; a world in which reason and science are the only guidelines for man's ethical choices. However, as Šatov points out, "reason [or science] has never had the power to define good and evil, or even to distinguish evil from good. . .; on the contrary it has always mixed them up in a shameful and pitiful way. (198-99) Thus Dostoevskij wishes to portray a world, which, based on reason and science, contains no absolute values of ethics or truth; a world in which "even the purest of heart" can "participate in the most monstrous villainy," and simultaneously "consider himself not as a villain."[28]

To create this apocalyptic vision, Dostoevskij uses a "human" witness-narrator, an inhabitant of such a world, and therefore incapable of presenting an omniscient, "absolutely true" point of view which would destroy the illusion of the world's all-pervasive relativity. Thus, Anton Lavrent'evič exhibits all the "human" weaknesses of those he describes. He is a liberal member of the intelligentsia, devoid of faith, who attempts to describe those "facts" he determines by his reason to be absolute truths: that is, a precise chronology of events, private conversations which he re-creates but is sure are true, and repeated descriptions which originate with him. Throughout, the narrator wishes to convince the reader that he can determine the truth of any given situation. It is as if he feels that by repeating his own evaluations he renders them absolutes. However, as Doložel points out, although the "Ich-form narrator assumes the role of constructing the narrative world," such a narrator has no "authentication authority," the world he creates is only "relatively authentic," and "it is not the world of absolute narrative facts."[29] Dostoevskij, seeking to depict the completely relative world of the apocalypse chooses to use the narrative mode that does not contain within itself, and thus cannot introduce into the novelistic world, an omniscient, absolute truth. The witness-narrator who is a character within that world becomes the most efficacious, if not the only, narrative frame which satisfies Dostoevskij's purpose.

Of course, Dostoevskij chooses his particular type of witness-narrator-authorial figure for many other reasons. Perhaps the most important of these is that by creating a narrator with authorial talents, Dostoevskij can allow him to plausibly present fully developed "round" characters or to "cloud" the depiction of Stavrogin and Petr Stepanovič, neither of whom he understands. However, these suggestions provide the framework for another paper on the effects achieved in the novel through its narrative mode.

NOTES

1. Such statements abound in the critical literature on the narrative. For example Percy Lubbock points out that the author's "sole thought is how to present the story, how to tell it in a way that will give the effect he desires. . . The only law that binds him throughout, whatever course he is pursuing, is the need to be consistent to *some* plan, to follow the principle he has adopted. . ." Percy Lubbock, *The Craft of Fiction* (New York: The Viking Press, 1957), 62, 71-72.

Norman Friedman expresses a similar view: "The question of effectiveness, therefore, is one of suitability of a given technique for the achievement of certain kinds of effects. . . The author-narrator. . . need not retire behind his work, so long as his point of view is adequately established and coherently maintained. It is a matter of consistency." Norman Friedman, "Point of View in Fiction: The Development of a Critical Concept," *The Theory of the Novel*, ed. Philip Stevick (New York: The Free Press, 1967), 132-133.

Wayne Booth remarks: "We all agree that point-of-view is in some sense a technical matter, a means to larger ends. . . Point-of-view should always be used 'consistently,' because otherwise the realistic illusion will be destroyed." Wayne C. Booth, "Distance and Point-of-View: An Essay in Classification," *The Theory of the Novel*, 89.

2. Friedman, 125.

3. Friedman, 125.

4. Friedman, 125.

5. Friedman, 126. Perhaps Dostoevskij's most vociferous, but typical Soviet critic is Ja. O. Zundelovič who charges: "It is impossible to distinguish the boundaries between the chronicler and the author, and the chronicler's narrative authority is often unexpectedly replaced by the author's; the chronicler himself appears before us as several different people. For this reason there is no unified 'prism' of refraction in *The Possessed* and the novel disintegrates into two unequal parts." Ja. O. Zundelovič, *Romany Dostoevskogo: Stat'i* (Taškent, 1963), 110.

Although Western critics, not having an ideological axe to grind with Dostoevskij, are usually less harsh in their condemnation of the novel's narrative structure, one can find detractors among them. Malcolm Jones, for example, avers that "this confusion of perspectives cannot help but undermine further the stability of the novel's [*The Possessed*'s] structure. By undermining the unity of point of view, Dostoevsky is threatening the ultimate foundation of narrative." Malcolm V. Jones, *Dostoevsky: The Novel of Discord* (London: Paul Elek, 1976), 147. Jones' comments are curiously negative since his central point is that Dostoevskij's works "are designed to convey the idea of disorder and their form reflects this endeavor" (17).

6. Sven Linner, *Dostoevskij on Realism* (Stockholm: Almquist & Wiksell, 1967), 67. Dostoevskij himself writing about *The Possessed* in his journal *Graždanin* indicates his concern with social truth and reality in the novel: "And why do you think the Nečaevs absolutely must be fanatics? They are very often merely swindlers. 'I am a swindler and not a socialist,' says one Nečaev in my novel *The Possessed;* but I assure you, he could have said it in real life. . . And do you really think that proselytes whom some Nečaev could have recruited among us necessarily must be good-for-nothings? I don't believe it, not at all; I myself am an old Nečaevite." F.,M. Dostoevskij, *Dnevnik pisatelja za 1873 god* (Pariž: YMCA Press), 356-357.

7. D. S. Lixačev, "'Letopisnoe vremja' u Dostoevskogo," *Poètika dɩevnorusskoj literatury,* 2nd ed. (Leningrad, 1971), 360.

8. Fyodor Dostoevsky, *The Notebooks for "The Possessed,"* ed. Edward Wasiolek, trans. Victor Terras (Chicago: The University of Chicago Press, 1968), 121. The translations have been checked against the original for accuracy.

9. Lixačev points out that Dostoevskij's purpose in creating his particular narrative mode in *The Possessed* is to "grasp the action, events, and individuals comprehensively; to reveal the facts from every side that they could be perceived," and therefore it is "important for Dostoevskij to create different points of view" (356). Lixačev is certainly correct that Dostoevskij presents many aspects of characters and facts through his narrative manner. However, if Dostoevskij were interested in this alone an "omniscient" narrator who willfully peers into the minds of the characters, circles his characters from an outside perspective giving various impressions, and even presents the thoughts of other characters about each other could certainly present a more comprehensively rounded characterization than any restricted "human" narrator. What Lixačev fails to realize in the narrative mode of *The Possessed* is that it is important for Dostoevskij to create a realistic character as narrator and that he gives him the authorial traits which allow him to present "round" characters. Thus Dostoevskij creates other characters despite and not necessarily because of his narrative choice.

10. Again Zundelovič is typical: "We will. . . linger over. . . the narrative changes of face and show that they are a stylistic indicator of the novel's flawed quality and its ideological and artistic defectiveness" (110). Malcolm Jones also expressed similar sentiments: "It might be argued that Dostoevskij was being inconsistent due to haste, or because his chosen narrative mode was not equal to the burden he wished to place upon it. There may be some truth in that" (147).

11. Fyodor Dostoevsky, *The Notebooks for "The Possessed,"* 121, 127.

12. Dostoevskij often refers to the narrator as an author in the notebooks: "How it all appeared to Liputin as he was trying to read Nechaev. The *author* describes all of these products of Liputin's *imagination,* as he addresses the public."

"That Nechaev, as such, is still a *fortuitous and isolated* individual. He only thinks that everybody who resembles him is like him — *Which is where he is wrong,* to the point of naiveté. . . *This is to be stated by the author."* Fyodor Dostoevsky, *The Notebooks for "The Possessed,"* 346, 349-350.

13. V. A. Tunimanov, "Rasskazčik v 'Besax' Dostoevskogo,' *Issledovanija po poètike i stilistike* (Leningrad, 1971), 135.

14. Malcolm Jones also reluctantly resorts to the suggestion that the narrator is a "novelist" as he struggles to explain the narrative technique of *The Possessed* (147): "The most striking example of the narrator in the guise of novelist. . . is probably the detailed description of events leading up to Kirillov's suicide. There is no plausible way of reconciling this with the role of objective chronicler."

15. Franz Stanzel, *Narrative Situations in the Novel,* trans. James P. Pusack (Bloomington: Indiana University Press, 1971), 60-61.

16. F. M. Dostoevskij, *Polnoe sobranie sočinenij* (30 vols.; Leningrad: AN SSSR, 1972), X, 166, 173. All further quotes from *The Possessed* will be taken from this volume. The page numbers will be indicated in parentheses at the end of each quote. All translations, although influenced by Constance Garnett, are my own.

17. Baxtin, for example, asserts that "Dostoevskij's narration is always narration without [temporal] perspective. Using a term from art criticism, we can say that there is no "perspective representation" of the hero and event in Dostoevskij's works. The narrator is in a relationship of immediate proximity to the hero and the event taking place. From this maximally close aperspective point of view he constructs his depiction of them. It is true that Dostoevskij's chroniclers write their notes after the events' conclusion from a seemingly apparent time perspective. For example, the narrator of *The Possessed* often says 'now when

everything is over,' 'now as we recall this,' and so on, but in fact he constructs his narrative without any significant time perspective. M. Baxtin, *Problemy poètiki Dostoevskogo,* 2nd ed. (Moscow, 1963), 302, 303.

Lixačev (358) asserts that the novel's narrator describes events "with a tight rein" (*na korotkom privode*) and that he "observes and pursues the events but without any detached perspective."

Tunimanov flatly states (113): "Dostoevskij's novel [*The Possessed*] is without [time] perspective (*besperspektiven*)."

18. See B. V. Tomaševskij, *Teorija literatury: Poètika,* 4th ed. (Moscow-Leningrad, 1928), 134-136.

19. F. M. Dostoevskij, *Polnoe sobranie sočinenij,* X, 7, 53, 120, 162, 173, 252, 267, 385, 498.

20. I am using Meir Sternberg's definition of "fictive present," that is, the first "time section" that the author finds important enough "to deserve full scenic treatment, [and] turns it, implicitly but clearly, into a conspicuous signpost, signifying that this is precisely the point in time that the author has decided. . . to make the reader regard as the beginning of the action proper." Meir Sternberg, *Expositional Modes and Temporal Ordering in Fiction* (Baltimore: Johns Hopkins University Press, 1978), 20. Dostoevskij's narrator takes care to impress on the reader when his precise chronology begins: "I will now enter upon a description of that somewhat strange incident with which my chronicle actually begins." F. M. Dostoevskij, *Polnoe sobranie sočinenij,* X, 53.

21. Of course, in any realistic chronology events which occur simultaneously must be related sequentially. However, the narrator of *The Possessed,* as part of his strict chronological structuring, usually informs the reader when simultaneity occurs. Thus, for example, he points out that while he, Liza, Stavrogin and others were on their way to Semen Jakovlevič's, it was "almost at the same time and certainly on the same day that the meeting between Stepan Trofimovič and Varvara Petrovna finally took place"; later the narrator points out that when Mar'ja Šatova arrived it was "towards eight o'clock in the evening (at the very time when 'our group' was meeting at Èrkel"'s and waiting. . . for Petr Stepanovič)," and later that evening the narrator informs the reader that Šatov "rushed straight to Kirillov's, this was probably before Petr Stepanovič's and Liputin's visit to Kirillov's."; then Šatov falls asleep and "two or three hours passed. In that time Verxovenskij and Liputin had had time to visit Kirillov." Later in the novel, during Stepan Trofimovič's last days, the narrator tells the reader they occurred at the same time as Šatov's murder: "I [the narrator] may remark that as yet no one had heard of Šatov's fate." F. M. Dostoevskij, *Polnoe sobranie sočinenij,* X, 262, 432, 435, 440, 506.

22. Meir Sternberg, 280.

23. Tunimanov presents a detailed examination of the narrator's method of ironic "debasing" of Stepan Trofimovič. However, we disagree with one of Tunimanov's basic assumptions (121) that "the simplest device for debasing Stepan Trofimovič's image is the direct contrast of the truth with the make-believe, of real and exact facts with fiction and the 'tutor's chatter.'" Tunimanov obviously considers the "human" narrator capable of presenting the "truth" of any situation. We, on the other hand, feel that the irony is created through the disparity between the "experiencing" and "narrating" perspectives, neither of which are, or can be considered absolute truths.

24. These contradictions and qualifications in the narrator's "narrating" perspective reinforce our contention that the narrator cannot present absolute, unqualifiable facts and assessments.

25. The narrator, re-creating Petr Stepanovič's conversation, rather immodestly has Petr Stepanovič consider him one of those "sensible" people who has described Petr Stepanovič as having "dropped from the sky."

26. Fyodor Dostoevsky, *The Notebooks for "The Possessed,"* 251.

27. Fyodor Dostoevsky, *The Notebooks for "The Possessed,"* 253.

28. F. M. Dostoevskij, *Dnevnik pisatelja za 1873 god,* 360.

29. Lubomir Doložel, "Truth and Authenticity in Narrative," *Poetics Today,* 1 (Spring, 1980), 17.

FOLK BELIEFS ABOUT THE UNCLEAN FORCE
IN *THE BROTHERS KARAMAZOV**

Linda J. Ivanits, The Pennsylvania State University

The now substantial body of scholarship on Dostoevskij and folklore leaves no doubt as to the importance of legends and beliefs which reflect Russian popular religion in his works.[1] Studies of *The Brothers Karamazov* (*Brat'ja Karamazovy*) have treated such topics as the function in the novel of spiritual songs about Saint Alexis "Man of God," Grušen'ka's story of the old woman in hell and the onion ("Lukovka"), and certain apocryphal legends about the end of the world and the coming of the anti-Christ.[2] Discussions of folk belief and superstition usually focus on the novel's incorporation of the peasant reverence for Mother Earth and, to a lesser degree, on allusions to ancient rites of ancestor worship.[3] However, one subject which has evoked very little attention is the presence in *The Brothers Karamazov* of imagery connected with the negative spirit world of folk belief, "the unclean force" (*nečistaja sila*). In its broad meaning "the unclean force" signified that part of the spirit world which the folk considered harmful to man, and it included devils ("the unclean force" in the narrow sense of the term), nature spirits, and such human and animal agents of the devil as sorcerers, witches, "changelings" (*oborotni*), and certain types of corpses.[4] In the nineteenth century notions about the activities of the unclean force were encountered at every juncture in popular lore: they entered into accounts of the creation of the world and into stories of temptation and sin; they offered explanations for natural calamities, poor harvests, illness, excessive drinking, familial discord — even for such simple household accidents as spinning mistakes.[5]

This study will investigate the presence and function of folk notions about the unclean force in *The Brothers Karamazov*. For the modern reader unfamiliar with the superstitions of the nineteenth-century Russian peasant, the frequent mention of the devil is probably the clearest indication of the presence of these notions. In addition, early pages of the novel contain many references to a form of hysterics which the folk considered possession (*klikušestvo*) and at least one hint that sorcery may be practiced in the town of the novel.[6] But these direct references to the unclean force just scratch the surface. If one views the novel against a background of ethnographic descriptions of peasant beliefs, it is possible to discern an extensive network of this imagery; and much of it occurs in such focal scenes as the murder of Fedor Pavlovič and the death of Father Zosima.

Several recent investigations of folklore in *The Brothers Karamazov* provide insights which are also valid for imagery relating to the unclean force. These studies demonstrate that Dostoevskij frequently uses folklore imagery in conjunction with such central religious themes as the meaning of suffering, justice, and resurrection. Consequently, it is hardly surprising that a folklore reference is seldom an entity unto itself. Instead it usually echoes or coexists with other religious imagery, particularly Biblical and hagiographic; and sometimes a single image or allusion has both a folkloric and a Christian referent. For example, to determine how the figure of Saint Alexis shapes the portrayal of Aleša Karamazov, the Soviet scholar V. E. Vetlovskaja finds it necessary to examine the oral tradition about the saint as well as the canonical Life (Poètika, 161-92). Elsewhere Vetlovskaja shows how number symbolism has both folkloric and Christian overtones ("Simvolika," passim). Perhaps the most often cited instance of this relationship between folkloric and Christian imagery is the novel's epigraph: "I tell you, most solemnly, unless a wheat grain falls on the ground and dies, it remains a single grain; but if it dies, it yields a rich harvest" (John 12:24). This New Testament passage, which foretells Christ's death and glorification, is clearly associated with the Christian theme of resurrection in The Brothers Karamazov. However, a number of commentators note that it is equally connected with the veneration of the earth as a life-giving and regenerative force.[7] Where feasible, the present study will suggest how imagery relating to the unclean force interacts with more traditional Christian imagery.

In The Brothers Karamazov folk notions about the unclean force constitute one of the factors in the representation of an expanded universe which includes not only the visible world, but, in Zosima's words, "mysterious other worlds" through which all things on earth have their origin and remain alive (XIV, 290). A number of critics have maintained that the novel supports this construct of the cosmos and refutes the environmentalist conception of a rational, Euclidean world by including events which are contrary to logical evidence (Dmitrij does not kill his father), by suggesting that individual lives can be transformed through grace (Aleša's conversion), by intimating that the dead continue to affect the living (Markel's influence on Zosima; Zosima's on Aleša), and by hinting that the devil participates in the activities of men.[8] Much discussion has been devoted to Dostoevskij's use of color imagery to imply the presence of heavenly or demonic forces; light suggests goodness and joy and always accompanies the mention of Christ; darkness signals evil.[9] This sense of a cosmic struggle between light and darkness, good and evil echoes the imagery of the Fourth Gospel in which Christ is called the "light that shines in the dark" (John 1:5), and, as Vetlovskaja points out, it approximates the vision of the world in the Lives of Saints (Poètika, 128). It may also reflect folk beliefs which represented the world as seething with evil spirits engaged in a perpetual campaign against man's moral and physical welfare (Maksimov, 2-5; Tokarev, 106). In folk notions evil or unclean spirits were often called "black" (černyj) or "dark" (temnyj), while God or angels were referred to as "bright" (svetlyj).[10] Moreover, it was widely believed that each individual had an angel on his right side and a devil on his left and that these two spirits struggled continuously for his soul (Kolčin, 55).

Folkloric representations of particular evil spirits are not always distinguishable from those of the Bible and the Lives of Saints, partly because popular beliefs blended Christian and pre-Christian notions. The popular visual image of the devil reflected the influence of Orthodox iconography: he was pictured as black and furry with a sharp head, horns, hooves, and a tail; and he was usually lame (Tokarev, 106). In *The Brothers Karamazov* alongside specifically Biblical references to the devil ("The Book of Job," XIV, 264-65; "The Temptation of Christ in the Wilderness," XIV, 229-37), one encounters a host of minor demons which seem to be those of the popular imagination: the devils which Fedor Pavlovič fears will drag him to hell with their hooks (XIV, 23-24); those which drag the old woman of Grušen'ka's legend to hell (XIV, 319); the devils which Lise and Aleša see in their dreams (XV, 23); and especially the sensuous demons with horns and tails which Ferapont exorcizes (XIV, 153-54). The means mentioned in the novel for warding off these evil spirits, the sign of the cross and a birch broom (XIV, 153-54; XV, 23; XIV, 303), are among those which the folk employed (Maksimov, 5; Tokarev, 126). The poor-relative devil of Ivan's nightmare deviates from the popular representation (though it was believed that the devil could assume human form, Tokarev, 106); yet later, in mentioning him to Aleša, Ivan renders him a bit more folkloric by claiming that he has a tail and by emphasizing that he goes to the baths (*v banju,* XV, 86). In folk belief the bathhouse was a favorite haunt of the unclean force (Pomeranceva, 118; Tokarev, 98).[11] The devil which Ivan imagines under the material evidence at Dmitrij's trial appears in his traditional guise with a tail (XV, 117).

The motif of lameness which occurs extensively in the novel is probably connected with the folk representation of a lame devil. The roster of lame or crippled people includes Lise, Iljuša's mother and sister, Mar'ja Kondrateevna's mother, a servant in Zosima's childhood home, Maksimov's wife, and Samsonov (XIV, 49, 180, 95, 261, 380, 333). In addition, Ivan's gait is unsteady when he leaves Aleša after reciting the story of the Grand Inquisitor, Grigorij limps during his attack of lumbago, Madame Xoxlakova suffers from a swollen foot, Ivan's devil complains of rheumatism, and even the saintly Zosima has weak legs (XIV, 241, 355; XV, 13, 74; XIV, 37). Thus, lameness is used in conjunction with both major and minor characters, with characters normally associated with grace (Zosima) as well as those linked to the devil (Lise, Ivan).[12] This motif serves to fuse the representation of human suffering with the suggestion of the presence of the devil, and its extensiveness suggests the pervasiveness of both. It stands as a sign of the imperfection of this world and possibly hints at the Biblical account of man's vulnerability after the Fall (Genesis 3). Folk notions specifically connect the devil's lameness with his fallen state: it was believed that he injured himself when he was cast from heaven (Maksimov, 6-7).

Other widespread beliefs about the devil may enter the narrative fabric of *The Brothers Karamazov.* According to folk notions, one of the favorite pastimes of the devil was leading a man to drink; the devil was also held responsible for such maladies as fevers and psychic ailments (Maksimov 13, 18; Tokarev, 100-02, 106). The heavy drinking of Fedor Pavlovič, Dmitrij, and Snegïrev and the *nadryv* of such characters as Katerina Ivanovna, Iljuša, Snegirev, and Ferapont may in part reflect these beliefs.[13] The place names "Mokroe" ("Wet") and "Ozernaja Ulica" ("Lake Street") may be connected to the notion that the unclean force resided primarily in swamps, lakes, and other bodies of water (Tokarev, 106; Maksimov, 5-6). Of course, water is a standard Christian symbol for rebirth through baptism. In the novel water is especially associated with the tears of repentance with which Zosima advocates watering the earth (XIV, 292). At the same time, hell is twice represented as a burning lake: in Grušen'ka's story of the onion (XIV, 319) and in the mention of the apocryphal tale of the Mother of God in hell ("Xoždenie bogorodicy po mukam," XIV, 225).[14] Critics have noted that the three ordeals (*mytarstva*) which Dmitrij suffers during his interrogation at Mokroe are thematically linked to the "Wandering of the Mother of God in Hell" and that they represent an inferno through which he passes prior to his symbolic rebirth with the dream of the babe (XIV, 412-57; Peace, 284). Golubov has further demonstrated that the events at Mokroe contain echoes of the Biblical accounts of Christ's crucifixion and descent into hell, and he notes that the legend of the harrowing of hell which Dmitrij's driver Andrej relates foreshadows the significance of these events (127-28).

A similar sort of convergence of folkloric and Biblical allusions occurs in the depiction of the Snegirev household. The placing of this residence on "Lake Street" associates it with both the water of rebirth and with the hell of folk notions and of the "Wandering of the Mother of God in Hell." The term "nečistyj vozdux" which Snegirev's wife uses for "bad breath" carries a dual meaning: it could equally signify an atmosphere filled with the unclean force, and it echoes the use of the popular "nečistyj dux" and "nečistyj" for "devil" elsewhere in the novel (XIV, 184, 44, 303).[15] The agonies of this miniature hell are severe: the family is impoverished, and Snegirev is a drunkard and a buffoon; his wife is feeble-minded and crippled; his daughter Nina is hunchbacked and crippled; and his other daughter is a rationalist and a fighter for women's rights. She is, in Snegirev's words, "not crippled, but far too clever."[16] But the focal point of this crowded, dark household is the icon corner under which the child Iljuša lies dying (XIV, 182, 485). It is Iljuša's symbolic connection with the figure of Christ (perhaps more evident after death when he is surrounded by twelve schoolboy-apostles, XV, 189) which gives this scene meaning: the suggestion is that imperceptibly in the midst of these torments and deformations the process of regeneration is taking place.[17]

Another instance in which imagery relating to the unclean force is interwoven with suggestions of the operation of grace is in the presentation of *klikušestvo*. This ailment was characterized by convulsions, barking, and howling which often occurred during the Liturgy. Victims were normally carried to the front of the church, and when the gifts were brought forward at the offertory, the howling ceased (Maksimov, 160-61). In the nineteenth century *klikuši* were a common sight at Russian monasteries, and it is quite natural that one should be included in the crowd outside Zosima's cell (XIV, 44).[18] By far the most important *klikuša* mentioned is Sof'ja Ivanovna, Fedor Pavlovič's second wife and the mother of Aleša and Ivan. Commentators generally consider Sof'ja Ivanovna one of Dostoevskij's humble, saintly women, many of whom bear the name "Sof'ja" as a sign of a mysterious connection with "holy wisdom" (Zander, 67-89). The influence Sof'ja Ivanovna exerts on Aleša seems to justify this understanding: his most precious memory from childhood is of his mother holding him toward the icon in the rays of the setting sun during one of her attacks (XIV, 18). Critics interpret this moment as one of particular grace for Aleša, a seed planted in his heart as a child to bear fruit later (Belknap, 48-49).

The narrator of *The Brothers Karamazov* gives a vivid and ethnographically precise description of *klikušestvo* in which three possible explanations are mentioned: (1) the peasant understanding of the disease as a form of possession; (2) the possibility that the disease is a pretense of lazy women to avoid work; (3) and a medical explanation according to which the ailment is the result of heavy work, difficult childbirth, and physical abuse (XIV, 44). In Sof'ja Ivanovna's case the origin is obscure. There is a suggestion that it is caused by Fedor Pavlovič's cruelty and sexual abuse (XIV, 13, 126); but her benefactress also mistreated her before her marriage, and there is a strong suggestion that she tried to hang herself (XIV, 14). In the presentation of *klikušestvo,* as in the presentation of Ivan's devil later, a plausible medical explanation is offered (abuse in one case, hallucinations in the other, XV, 69-70), yet, at the same time care is taken not to rule out supernatural intervention. One has to reckon with the possibility that one of Dostoevskij's saints is possessed.

In *The Brothers Karamazov* imagery pertaining to the unclean force serves to implicate the devil extensively in the moral and physical agonies of both major characters (Ivan, for instance) and of characters who receive only the slightest mention (Maksimov's wife). The devil and suffering are so pervasive as to suggest that the hell of traditional notions, marked by various tortures and the presence of demons, may belong more specifically to this life than to an afterlife. Perhaps this is why Zosima shifts the understanding of hell from the usual conception of an eternal fire to the mystical notion of an inability to love (XIV, 292). The awesome power which the devil is granted in the lives of men, irrespective of their virtue or wickedness, leads directly to Ivan's question about the justice of a God who allows innocent children to suffer, for this question also pertains to the Snegirevs or Sof'ja Ivanovna.[19] It is significant that Zosima recapitulates Ivan's query in mentioning abusive reactions to Job's sufferings: "How could God hand over his most beloved saint to the caprice of the devil, take his children from him, smite him with sickness and sores so that he cleansed the pus from his wounds with a potsherd. . .? " (XIV, 265). Zosima's response is that the greatness of this story lies in the mystery through which passing earthly reality and eternal truth are brought together (XIV, 265).

The novel does not offer a logical explanation for suffering. But, partly through thematic parallels between folkloric allusions to the unclean force and Biblical references to the devil, it imbues suffering with meaning. The specific moments mentioned in the life of Job — joy in his family and possessions, physical agonies, bereavement, the temptation to curse God — stand as archetypal human experiences which are repeated with varying degrees of completeness in the lives of the characters in the novel.[20] They are also present in the events noted in the life of Christ: joy at the wedding in Cana, temptation by the devil in the wilderness, torture and crucifixion (XIV, 325-27; 229, 224). But the stories of Job and Christ end not in defeat, but salvation: Job's new family and wealth, Christ's resurrection. There are hints that like these Biblical figures, the victims of the unclean force in the novel will find deliverance. Side by side with imagery suggestive of the devil's presence stands imagery indicative of the operation of grace: the ray of light during Sof'ja Ivanovna's attack, the icon lamp above the dying Iljuša.

Considering the major role accorded to the devil, one might expect to find allusions to the unclean force surrounding the central event in the plot of *The Brothers Karamazov,* the murder of Fedor Pavlovič. During his interrogation at Mokroe, Dmitrij claims in a burst of passion that the devil killed his father (XIV, 429). In truth, the links between the murderer Smerdjakov and the devil are uncannily strong, and this is especially evident in the story of his origin. In the narrative of Smerdjakov's birth and naming folklore motifs are interwoven with Biblical and sectarian imagery. He is the son of "Stinking Lizaveta," an idiot girl regarded as a holy fool,[21] who has been raped probably by Fedor Pavlovič and possibly by a convict named Karp. When it is time for her delivery, Lizaveta escapes from the watchful eye of the merchant widow Kondrat'eva, mysteriously climbs the high fence surrounding the Karamazov yard, and makes her way to the bathhouse. The birth of Smerdjakov coincides with the death of the infant son of Grigorij. This child was born with six fingers and was cursed by his father who, considering him a dragon, asked that he not be baptized. He was, however, baptized, and immediately afterwards fell ill and died. When Smerdjakov was born, Grigorij handed him to Marfa to nurse saying, "A child of God and an orphan is kin to us all. . . Our little dead one sent this, who came from the devil's son and a righteous woman" (XIV, 92-93). Smerdjakov was christened "Pavel" to which "Fedorovič" was soon added. Fedor Pavlovič had no objections to a patronymic implicating him in paternity, and he himself coined the surname after the nickname of the child's mother, "Stinking" (Smerdjaščaja, XIV, 90-93).

The story of Smerdjakov's birth and naming seems to be a play with the Biblical paradigm for the birth of a special child through the intervention of the supernatural (for example, the Old Testament narratives of the births of Ishmael and Isaac and the New Testament narratives of the birth of John the Baptist and Christ, Genesis 16:1-16; Genesis 21:1-7; Luke 1:5-25; Luke 1:26-38).[22] This is particularly suggested by Grigorij's formulaic "child of God" and "who came from a righteous woman." In Smerdjakov's case, however, it is not only God that is mentioned, but also the devil, and the implication is that this child bears ominous forebodings. This is further suggested by the naming ceremony. In the Biblical patterns the child's name is linked to his mission (Genesis 16:11-12; Genesis 17:20-21; Luke 1:14-17; Luke 1:32-33). Smerdjakov's name, a reversal of that of Fedor Pavlovič, associates him with the baseness of his probable father; his last name points to his moral stench.

It is not entirely clear who "the devil's son" of Grigorij's formula is. On the one hand it may be Fedor Pavlovič, who earlier in the novel calls himself the "father of lies," a Biblical epithet for Satan (XIV, 41; Belknap, 35). Yet, it could also refer to Karp, whose significance may be that his name links him to the founder of one of the first Russian sects (Fedotov, II, 113-14). Other sectarian imagery can be found in this narrative: Grigorij is interested in the Flagellants (*xlysty*) after the birth of his deformed child, and the widow Kondrat'eva who keeps Lizaveta during her pregnancy bears the telling name of Kondratij Selivanov, the founder of the sect of Castrates (*skopcy*) with whom Smerdjakov is later connected (XIV, 89, 92, 115).[23] The distortion of the Biblical paradigm acquires a more specific meaning viewed against sectarian belief in the periodic reincarnation of Christs, Madonnas, prophets, and prophetesses.[24] The rape of Lizaveta may contain overtones of the orgies (known among sectarians as "Christly love") in which sectarian holy women conceived (Mel'nikov-Pečerskij, 356-57).

The folklore imagery in the narration of Smerdjakov's birth intensifies the suggestion that the child is associated with the powers of evil. The bathhouse as an "unclean" place has already been mentioned.[25] Among the peasantry it was believed that at the time of birth threat of attack from the unclean force was particularly severe. Every precaution was taken to guard the mother and the newborn baby: the sign of the cross was made on doors and windows; holy candles were lit; the ceiling was beat with a broom; and the mother and child were kept away from strangers.[26] The story of the death of Grigorij's son and the birth of Smerdjakov seems to contain an allusion to one of the most widespread superstitions about the harm which the unclean force inflicts: the substitution of a devil child for a human one. According to this belief, unbaptized children were the most susceptible; a curse (such as, "May the forest spirit carry you off!"), a careless word, or an evil desire were all that was needed to bring about this misfortune (Maksimov, 20-21).

Smerdjakov seems to fulfill the purpose for which he was born when he serves as the agent for the murder of Fedor Pavlovič. As Peace notes, this connection between his birth and the murder is made explicit when Dmitrij climbs the fence in the same place as Lizaveta and when Marfa thinks of Lizaveta

upon hearing Grigorij moan (XIV, 353, 409; Peace, 260). Other imagery connected with the unclean force surrounds the murder: it takes place in a chapter
entitled "In the Dark" ("V temnote"), and it is only now that Grigorij limps.
Particularly significant is Marfa's healing of Grigorij's lumbago: the details of the
cure indicate that she is employing witch-doctoring (*znaxarstvo*), a practice not
always distinguishable from sorcery (*koldovstvo*), though in theory the witch
doctor did not have dealings with the unclean force (Tokarev, 22-23). Marfa
adds secret grasses to vodka and whispers a prayer while administering the
potion. Very often the folk used the term "prayer" (*molitva*) in the sense of
"charm" (*zagovor*).[27] This cure has the functional purpose of creating conditions
in which Smerdjakov is willing to risk murder, and its importance is underscored
by the number of times it is repeated: Smerdjakov tells Ivan in asking him to go
to Čermašnja; the narrator mentions it in "In the Dark"; and it is mentioned at
Dmitrij's trial (XIV, 247, 355; XV, 46, 97-98).

It may also be possible to detect in the events surrounding the murder
allusions to the folk belief in the constant struggle between an individual's
guardian angel and the devil. Dmitrij claims that his guardian angel, his mother's
prayers, and God kept him from commiting the murder (XIV, 355, 425-426,
428), and at one point he uses the popular "bright spirit" (*dux svetlyj*) for
"angel" (XIV, 425-26). Ivan's swaying gait connects him with the devil through
the suggestion of lameness (XIV, 241).[28] It may also hint that he is in the throes
of a spiritual conflict. Moreover, it is the devil who wins this bout, for immediately afterwards Ivan authorizes the murder of his father by telling Smerdjakov
that he will leave the next day (XIV, 249).

Finally, folk notions about the unclean force and hagiographic motifs are
interwoven in the presentation of the corruption of Zosima's body and the
non-corruption of Iljuša's. According to the tradition of the Lives of Saints
bodily preservation and the emission of a sweet fragrance are testimonies of
special holiness; on the other hand, ancient notions about the earth demand
bodily decay. It was believed that the earth accepted nothing unclean, and
failure to decompose was considered an indication of sinfulness or a connection
with the unclean force.[29] Thus, while the hagiographic tradition interprets
Zosima's rapid decomposition as a denial of sainthood, the folkloric one considers it a sign of a special acceptance by Mother Earth — perhaps a reward for
his veneration of the earth in his lifetime. Just the opposite is true in Iljuša's
case: in the tradition of the Lives, the failure of his body to decompose is
evidence of sanctity. But folkloric motifs surrounding the presentation of his
death suggest a connection with the unclean force.

Iljuša had asked to be buried on the edge of a field by a stone to which he
and his father often walked. Just prior to the funeral, Snegirev says that he
intends to carry out Iljuša's wish, but the landlady protests claiming that it
would be wrong to bury the child by a "vile" (*poganyj*) stone as if he had been
strangled (*udavlennik,* XV, 191). The word "poganyj" had overtones of "pagan"

and "unclean" (Dal', *Tolkovyj slovar'*, III, 153), and "udavlennik" specifies a sub-category of corpse considered by the folk unclean. Included among such deceased (called as a whole *založnye*) were suicides, those who died violent deaths, and those who died prematurely. According to popular superstition, the bodies of these dead were not accepted by the earth, and they were destined to walk the earth until they completed the lifetime assigned to them at birth (Zelenin, 1-2). Russian peasants distinguished sharply between the unclean dead and "ancestors" (*roditeli*), and they preferred to bury *založnye* away from ancestral cemeteries. In some places the unclean dead were buried on the edge of fields (Zelenin, 18).

In the presentations of the deaths of Father Zosima and Iljuša the hagiographic and folkloric signs function in such a way as to suggest contradictory interpretations: within the tradition of the Lives, Zosima is denied and Iljuša is granted sainthood, but in the folkloric schema Iljuša's corpse is unclean while Zosima's bears the mark of special acceptance by the earth. In a sense, these two sets of signs nullify each other, and rightly so, for they are "stumbling blocks," the sort of false material proof of eternal things which contradicts free faith. The desire of such characters as Ferapont to stamp Zosima (or Iljuša) "saint" or "sinner" runs counter to Zosima's maxim that one man cannot judge another (XIV, 291), and, more importantly, it shifts attention away from the true meaning of death. Over and above these signs stands the promise of Job and Christ, made explicit in the Biblical epigraph, that new life springs from death. Zosima and Iljuša are "wheat grains" whose death heralds an "abundant harvest." Moreover, the continuity of Zosima's work in Aleša and the precious memory which Iljuša gives the boys are indications that their regenerative work has already begun.

Throughout this discussion we have tried to show how the incorporation of popular beliefs about the unclean force in *The Brothers Karamazov* touches upon the central questions of suffering, justice, and resurrection and how these folkloric notions interact with more traditional Christian imagery. It is significant that a synthesis between pre-Christian and Christian imagery is evident in the very final note to the novel. The speech at Iljuša's stone expresses the Christian hope of resurrection and, at the same time, mentions ancient rites of ancestor worship (the funeral meal) which the Church had assimilated. Aleša explains to the boys on their way to Iljuša's funeral meal that they should not be disturbed at eating pancakes (*bliny*) for this is a custom which is ancient, eternal, and good (XV, 197).

NOTES

* Earlier versions of this study were read at the annual meeting of AATSEEL in December 1977 and at the annual meeting of the Pennsylvania Folklore Society in April 1978.

1. See, for example, George Gibian, "Dostoevskij's Use of Russian Folklore," *Journal of American Folklore,* 69 (1956), 239-53; L. M. Lotman, "Romany Dostoevskogo i russkaja legenda," *Russkaja literatura,* 15 (1972), No. 2, 129-41; N. K. Piksanov, "Dostoevskij i fol'klor," *Sovetskaja ètnografija,* No. 1-2 (1934), 152-65; and R. Pletnev, "La légende chrétienne dans l'oeuvre de Dostoïevsky," *Études slaves et est-européennes,* 6 (Fall-Winter 1961), Parts 3-4, 131-57.

2. See V. E. Vetlovskaja, "Dostoevskij i poetičeskij mir drevnej Rusi: Literaturnye i fol'klornye istočniki *Brat'ev Karamazovyx,"* in *Issledovanija po istorii russkoj literatury XI-XVII vv.,* Vol. 28 of *Trudy otdela drevnerusskoj literatury* (Leningrad: Nauka, 1974), 300-307, *Poètika romana* Brat'ja Karamazovy (Leningrad: Nauka, 1977), 161-92, and "Simvolika čisel v *Brat'jax Karamazovyx,"* in *Drevnerusskaja literatura i russkaja kul'tura XVIII-XX vv.,* Vol. 26 of *Trudy otdela drevnerusskoj literatury* (Leningrad: Nauka, 1971), 139-50. See also Piksanov, 161-62 and Pletnev, "La légende," 153-55.

3. See, for example, Roger Anderson, "Mythical Implications of Father Zosima's Religious Teachings," *Slavic Review,* 38 (June 1979), No. 2, 280-89; Vyacheslav Ivanov, *Freedom and the Tragic Life: A Study in Dostoevsky,* tr. Norman Cameron (New York: Noonday, 1957), 41-45; R. V. Pletnev, "Zemlja," in *O Dostoevskom,* ed. A. L. Bem (Prague: Legiografie, 1929), I, 153-62; V. E. Vetlovskaja, "Tvorčestvo Dostoevskogo v svete literaturnyx i fol'klornyx parallelej: 'Stroitel'naja žertva'," in *Mif-fol'klor-literatura,* ed. V. G. Bazanov (Leningrad: Nauka, 1978), 109-13; and L. A. Zander, *Dostoevsky,* tr. Natalie Duddington (London: SCM Press, 1948), 36-65.

4. See S. V. Maksimov, *Nečistaja sila. Nevedomaja sila,* in *Sobranie sočinenij* (20 Vols.; SPb.: Samoobrazovanie, 1908-13), XVIII, 3-206 and S. A. Tokarev, *Religioznye verovanija vostočnoslavjanskix narodov XIX-načala XX v.* (Moscow and Leningrad: AN SSSR, 1957), 79, 99-100, and elsewhere.

5. See Ė. V. Pomeranceva, *Mifologičeskie personaži v russkom fol'klore* (Moscow: Nauka, 1975), 28-154; A. Kolčin, "Verovanija krest'jan Tul'skoj gubernii," *Ètnografičeskoe obozrenie,* 11 (1899), No. 3, 1-60; A. I. Ivanov, "Verovanija krest'jan Orlovskoj gub.," *Ètnografičeskoe obozrenie,* 12 (1900), No. 4, 68-118; D. Ušakov, "Materialy po narodnym verovanijam velikorussov," *Ètnografičeskoe obozrenie,* 8 (1896), No. 2-3, 146-204; Maksimov, 3-28, 51-57, 71-159, and elsewhere; and Tokarev, 20-43, 79-110, 120-21.

6. F. M. Dostoevskij, *Brat'ja Karamazovy,* Vols. XIV and XV of *Polnoe sobranie sočinenij* (30 Vols. promised, Leningrad: Nauka, 1976), XIV 13, 23-24, 44, 47, 153-54, and elsewhere. All further reference to *The Brothers Karamazov* will be to this edition and will be indicated in the text. Translations are my own.

The mention of sorcery occurs in a conversation between Zosima and one of his penitents, the widow Proxorovna. Bedrjagina, a rich merchant woman, had advised Proxorovna to enter her missing son's name in church for the office of the dead so that "his soul will be disturbed and he will write home." When Proxorovna aska Zosima about this practice, he claims that to pray for a living person as if he were dead is similar to sorcery (*koldovstvo,* XIV, 47).

7. See Richard Peace, *Dostoyevsky: An Examination of the Major Novels* (Cambridge, England: Cambridge Univ. Press, 1971), 285 and Anderson, 279-280. The interweaving of folkloric and Christian motifs is especially pronounced in Zosima's teachings. It is interesting to compare Anderson's study of these teachings in terms of mythic elements with

another recent study of thematic parallels between Zosima's last conversations and the farewell discourse of Christ in the Fourth Gospel. See Alexander Golubov, "Religious Imagery in the Structure of *The Brothers Karamazov*," in *Russian and Slavic Literature,* ed. Richard Freeborn et als. (Cambridge, Mass.: Slavica, 1976), 116-20.

8. The most detailed discussion of the way in which the plot of *The Brothers Karamazov* serves to refute the theory of environment as advanced by the Russian radical intelligentsia of the 1860's and to support the construct of an expanded universe is probably that of Vetlovskaja in *Poètika,* 143-61 and elsewhere. See also Ralph E. Matlaw, The Brothers Karamazov: *Novelistic Technique* (The Hague: Mouton, 1957), 23; Nathan Rosen, "Style and Structure in *The Brothers Karamazov:* The Grand Inquisitor and The Russian Monk," *Russian Literature Triquarterly,* I (Fall 1971), 361-63; and Zander, 15-34.

9. For example, Robert Belknap, *The Structure of* The Brothers Karamazov (The Hague and Paris: Mouton, 1967), 48 and Matlaw, 30-31.

10. See Vladimir Dal', *Tolkovyj slovar' živogo velikorusskogo jazyka* (4 Vols., 2nd ed., SPb.: M. O. Vol'f), I, 157-58; II, 542-43; IV, 597. See also the creation legend reported by Kolčin (53-55) in which God is called "svetlyj" and the devil "temnyj." G. P. Fedotov sees in such creation legends the only evidence of the Bogomil heresy on Russian folk beliefs, *The Russian Religious Mind* (2 Vols. Cambridge, Mass.: Harvard Univ. Press, 1964), I, 354.

11. By the time *The Brothers Karamazov* was written, the bathhouse had already acquired the status of a symbol of hell in Dostoevskij's art. See Moisej Al'tman, "Čitaja Dostoevskogo," *Bulletin* of the International Dostoevsky Society, No. 7, 1977, 113-14.

12. For a discussion of the ways in which various characters are associated with either divine grace or the devil see Belknap, 47-50 and 34-41. The most detailed investigation of Ivan's links to the devil is probably that of Vetlovskaja in *Poètika.* Vetlovskaja argues that Ivan serves as the devil's surrogate in his tavern conversation with Aleša and that Ivan's illness is in fact possession (98-102 and elsewhere).

13. For a discussion of *nadryv* in *The Brothers Karamazov* see Edward Wasiolek, *Dostoevsky: The Major Fiction* (Cambridge, Mass.: M. I. T. Press, 1964), 160 and Belknap, 45-47.

14. For a detailed discussion of the function of "The Wandering of the Mother of God in Hell" in the novel, see Vetlovskaja, "Dostoevskij i poetičeskij mir drevnej Rusi." Vetlovskaja suggests that Dostoevskij substituted "burning lake" as an image of hell for the "burning river" of the actual legends in order to suit his novelistic purpose, 298.

15. There is some evidence that Snegirev's wife is to be understood as a holy fool (*jurodivaja*): in calling Aleša "Černomazov" rather than "Karamazov" she reveals the significance of his name ("čern-" is the Russian root for "black"; "kara-" the Turkish one, Matlaw, 31). Her strange utterances also point to the problem of distinguishing good from evil, and they may contain a prediction of Zosima's putrefaction (XIV, 184). For a discussion of the holy fool see Fedotov, II, 316-43.

16. A number of studies have noted the relationship between the devil and intellectuality in Dostoevskij's art. See R. Pletnev, "O duxax zla i d'javola u Dostoevskogo i Tolstogo," *Novyj žurnal,* 119 (1975), 94 and Eliseo Vivas, "The Two Dimensions of Reality in *The Brothers Karamazov*," in *Dostoevsky: A Collection of Critical Essays,* ed. Rene Wellek (Englewood Cliffs, N. J.: Prentice-Hall, 1962), 83.

17. For a discussion of imagery connecting Iljuša with Christ see Rimvydas Silbajoris, "The Children in *The Brothers Karamazov*," *Slavic and East European Journal,* VII (1963), No. 1, 37.

18. For a lengthy discussion of *klikušestvo* from a medical point of view see N. V. Krainskij, *Porča, klikuši, i besnovatye, kak javlenija russkoj narodnoj žizni* (Novgorod: Gubernskaja tipografija, 1900). Krainskij notes the connection in the popular imagination between *klikušestvo* and sorcery: in their howling, the afflicted called out the names of the

sorcerers who "spoiled" them (49, 180). He also notes the frequency of *klikuši* in the Simonov monastery near Moscow; apparently a certain Father Mark had devised a six-week cure for afflicted women (182). A concise synopsis of Krainskij's medical investigations is contained in the last chapter (213-43). Interestingly, he maintains that though in some cases the affliction was feigned, in many cases it was genuine.

19.   Here it is impossible to discuss in detail the mechanisms of the "debate" in the novel between the Grand Inquisitor and the Russian Monk, a debate which has left critics divided as to whose side the novel really supports. For a discussion of this problem and a synopsis of critical attitudes see Rosen and Wasiolek, 161-79.

20.   Anderson notes that Zosima's understanding of the story of Job illustrates his mythic conception of time, 282.

21.   Normally the madness of the holy fool was feigned (Fedotov, II, 317). Lizaveta's expression of complete idiocy indicates that she may not be a genuine *jurodivaja* (XIV, 90).

22.   For an interesting discussion of the way in which Old Testament narratives for the birth of a special child shaped the New Testament ones see Raymond E. Brown, *The Birth of the Messiah: A Commentary on the Infancy Narratives in Matthew and Luke* (Garden City, New York: Doubleday, 1977), 73-74 and elsewhere.

23.   Peace discusses the affinities between Smerdjakov and the Castrates at length, yet, for some reason, he makes almost no reference to sectarian imagery in this nativity story (260-63).

24.   See P. I. Mel'nikov-Pečerskij, "Tajnye sekty" and "Belye golubi" in Vol. 6 of *Polnoe sobranie sočinenij* (14 Vols. SPb.: Marks, 1909), 251-422.

25.   It was in fact common for Russian peasant women to give birth in the bathhouse. See Sula Benet, tr. and ed. *The Village of Viriatino: An Ethnographic Study of a Russian Village from before the Revolution to the Present* (Garden City, New York: Doubleday, 1970), 119.

26.   See A. Red'ko, "Nečistaja sila v sud'bax ženščiny-materi," *Ètnografičeskoe obozrenie*, 11 (1899), No. 1-2, 77.

27.   For discussions of charms and witch doctors see Vladimir Dal', *O pover'jax, sueverijax i predrassudkax russkogo naroda*, 2nd ed. (SPb. and Moscow: M. O. Vol'f, 1880), 32-50, 65-79, and Maksimov, 184-96.

28.   Vetlovskaja also connects Ivan's gait with the representation of the lame devil, *Poètika*, 99.

29.   D. K. Zelenin, *Očerki russkoj mifologii, I: Umeršie neestesvennoj smert'ju i rusalki* (Petrograd: A. V. Orlov, 1916), 6.